Restless
Journey

Marcus Ryan

HARVEST HOUSE PUBLISHERS

EUGENE, OREGON

Cover photos © Photos.com

Cover by Koechel Peterson & Associates, Inc., Minneapolis, Minnesota

RESTLESS JOURNEY
Copyright © 2006 by Marcus Ryan
Published by Harvest House Publishers
Eugene, Oregon 97402
www.harvesthousepublishers.com

Library of Congress Cataloging-in-Publication Data

Ryan, Marcus, 1957-
  Restless journey / Marcus Ryan.
    p. cm.
  ISBN-13: 978-0-7369-1735-3 (pbk.)
  ISBN-10: 0-7369-1735-7
  1. Christian men—Religious life. 2. Interpersonal relations—Religious aspects—Christianity. I. Title.
  BV4528.2.R93 2006
  248.8'42—dc22   2005024741

Printed in the United States of America

06 07 08 09 10 11 12 13 14 / LB-KB / 10 9 8 7 6 5 4 3 2 1

*This book is dedicated
to my late father, Arthur.*

Acknowledgments

There is no way to overstate the role others played in the writing of this book. From the beginning to the end, others guided, shaped, and influenced its direction and helped transform it from an idea to a finished manuscript.

I must express my gratitude to Harvest House Publishers, and its president, Bob Hawkins, Jr., for taking a chance with me, a new author, and for giving this project the attention they did. Your commitment was evident in the work and support of V.P. of editorial, Carolyn McCready, and V.P. of sales, John Constance. I'd also like to thank Gene Skinner, the copy and structure editor, who smoothed the rough spots and helped bring the message into focus. But my deepest gratitude to the great people at Harvest House is reserved for Terry Glaspey, who took what was perhaps an interesting but vague idea and hand-carried it from that point to its completion.

I owe a profound debt to a few men who spent countless hours walking through the first drafts of the chapters. Each of these men—Jon Sterns, Victor Conkle, Mark Sterns, John Watkins, Mike Newton, and Chuck Romer—plays a unique role in my life and constantly provokes me to continue the struggle to become the man he believes God made me to be. I hope that, to some degree, I do the same for each of them. I am a better man because of their decades-long influence on my life.

God also brought new friends into my life over the past few years. These men continue to show me how much I need friendships. A big, heartfelt thanks to Tom Howard and David Schober for your help through the hardest period of writing this book, and to Mark Baldwin, Dale Weller, Phil Madeira, Brian Connor, Tim Reynolds, and Jim Chaffee for your encouragement and support.

Also, without the insights and heart checks of Kim Newton, Paula Sterns, Karen Conkle, and Kitty Sterns this book would have missed the mark in certain key places. I found it interesting that a book *for* men written *by* a man still needed the understanding nod of certain women.

Lastly, and most importantly, I must thank my incredible family. Before, during, and after the writing of this manuscript my daughters Quinlyn, Elle, and Madelin prayed for me, listened to me, laughed with me, questioned me, and gave up time that should have gone to them. And to my wife, Lisa, I formally apologize for spending time writing during our first-ever anniversary getaway. That being said, you are the best hearth and editor a man has ever been given. Why God guided you to marry me I'll never know, but I'm a different man because of you.

Contents

1

THE END

Death will come when it will come.
Hamlet
BY WILLIAM SHAKESPEARE

....

As FUNERALS GO, this one was pretty well attended. The man in the casket was a small-screen star some years back, appearing in a number of sitcoms in the '60s and '70s. Although he had long since vanished from the public eye, baby boomers occasionally recognized him. In his heyday, his manager convinced him to invest the money he made in television into real estate in the San Fernando Valley, so at the time of his death he was also fairly wealthy.

Few people considered him old because he always looked healthy, and as a result, everyone who knew him was surprised when he went to sleep one night and never woke up. The doctor said he had an aneurism deep in his brain and probably died very quickly.

On the front row of the dark chapel sat the man's current wife, his fourth. She was considerably younger than he was, and the two had lived apart for most of the last year. Seated just behind her was a daughter from his first marriage, but none of the other seven children from his previous marriages showed up. Neither did any of his former wives. Not even his first, though he had been married to her for more than 20 years. His lawyer was there.

Several of the cast members from his TV days and a guy he played golf with now and then made it to the funeral. Three of the former cast members got up and made brief comments, generally talking about characters he had played in the sitcoms. They drew quite a bit of laughter when they imitated phrases and expressions he had invented for some of his more memorable characters. The priest commented on the laughter the man had brought to millions and his generosity to certain charitable causes.

Near the end of the 45-minute ceremony, I began to feel a little uncomfortable. I'd listened to person after person talk about roles and characters, and we all remembered funny episodes and bloopers, but by the end of the funeral I had learned little about this man. I heard about the characters he played, but the funeral service provided little more than a view from the grandstands as he walked the red carpet of life. I felt as if I were watching a compilation of reruns on TV. Even his wife talked about things I had read in the newspapers.

Where were the stories from his children? How about memories his wife had that would give me insight into the man? No one mentioned any brothers or sisters, although I'd read that he had a brother and two sisters. Who were his friends? Not costars who knew him as the same characters I did, but longtime friends who would tell us about this man's heart, his faith, his fears?

I began to wonder if *anyone* really knew him. We all knew he was wealthy. He was a husband and father. He was respected in his field. He was recognized in his community. But who was he when the camera was off, when he put aside the familiar masks of the characters he had created? Did he hide who he really was, or did he just lose sight of himself? The dressing room of our mind will only hold so many people, so perhaps his real self simply excused itself from the room because the man favored the characters he played more than the person he was.

For all his wealth and fame, I couldn't help but feel a loss for a man who never lived. We celebrated the lives of TV characters but barely mentioned the man in the casket. Later, as the cars pulled away from the cemetery and the workers lowered the body into the ground, I found myself thinking, *Who was that man in the casket?*

The End of Your Life

Have you stopped to consider that your funeral will be your last event in this life? It is the end of the presence of your body among the living. At that point, whatever you were aiming for, whatever you had as life goals, whatever you considered as important will reach its end. All that you've done, owned, and experienced in life will be finished. Your possessions will be in someone else's hands. Your job and other roles will be over.

Picture yourself in an open casket at the front of a large room. Suppose for a moment that as you lie there you are somehow aware of what is going on in the room around you. You hear music and the sound of people as they move step-by-step down the hardwood floors. You also detect the quiet muffled sound of whispering. You have reached the end of what some call the game of life. You can change nothing, and you have nothing left to do. As you wait for the funeral service to start, you can't help but wonder how you did. You feel almost as if you're waiting for a verdict or a score from the judges.

In the 2004 Olympics in Athens, a sharp-shooting athlete was one shot from an Olympic gold medal. Leading after nine shots, he needed only to hit the target anywhere near the bulls-eye to win the gold. He had spent his life preparing for this moment, and his confidence level was high.

The expert rifleman aimed at the target, took a deep breath, relaxed his body, and squeezed off the shot. It was straight and true and hit its mark exactly. He paused and waited for the judges to declare him the winner. There was only one problem. He had hit the bulls-eye of the wrong target.

The shooter inadvertently aimed one lane over and made an expert shot at the wrong goal. Although he hit exactly what he was aiming for, his score for that round was a zero, and he dropped from a certain gold medal to eighth place. He had been prepared, dedicated, and certain. But none of that mattered. He might as well have fired the shot into the air. No second chance, no do-overs. The event was over.

Who Were You?

Shortly after you have passed from the world you've known to the world unknown, your friends and family will set aside a few minutes just for you. In that brief period of time, they will sum up your life. Most funerals are short, generally lasting less than half an hour. Doesn't it seem strange that your life could be memorialized in such a wisp of time?

While a fat résumé might be an impressive part of the ceremony, the professional honors and accolades begin to seem trite next to the personal stories and anecdotes your family and friends will share. This is where the persona attached to the résumé crumples like yellowed, brittle parchment and gives way to the person that people knew you to be. Your last words may be mentioned. Someone will probably talk about the last time he saw you. A couple of people will be asked to say a few words because family or friends thought they were the ones who knew you best.

You lie and wait. Who is there? What will they say? Who isn't there? Why? You squeezed off your shot, and it's out of your hands. It is time for those you knew, and those who knew you, to review your life.

Six Men to Carry My Casket

Absent some sort of "you have three months to live" edict from a doctor, most of us take life in stride and figure the end will take care of itself. When it does come, it often comes out of nowhere: You leave for work one morning but never return home. William Shakespeare was right on point when he wrote in *Hamlet* that death will come when it will come, and a man has little to say about it.

One morning I was having coffee with a longtime friend at a little bakery in downtown Franklin, Tennessee. My friend told me about a conference he had just attended where a guy was talking about why he left the church he had been attending. Apparently the man looked around one Sunday morning at church and realized he didn't even know six guys who could carry his casket if he died. All the programs and activities at the church didn't matter if he didn't really know a few men and if they didn't know him well enough to walk alongside his casket. So he left.

One can hardly blame him. Men are consumed with providing for their families, and the chore of keeping up with the stress of daily life can be exhausting. Every day you face changing demands at home, at work, and even in your own body. But one thing doesn't really change. While men function pretty well alone on a day-to-day basis, no one wants to be alone when he dies.

The man who left the church because he didn't know six men who would carry his casket wasn't making the decision to leave because he faced imminent death. Presumably he had no foreknowledge of when he was going to die. Comedian Steven Wright said he knows when he is going to die because his birth certificate has an expiration date on it, but really, none of us know when and how the end will come. This man looked ahead and concluded that a future certainty required an immediate correction in his life course.

The Rules of Life

Of course, some people never realize that what they are doing isn't working. They live in blissful ignorance. Others sense the void but assume they just need more of the same...more money, more sex, more stuff. They may blame the hollowness on those around them: *If only I had a different wife or a different boss, or I lived in a different city.*

However, the largest group of men just keep plugging along. They sense a hole in their lives, but they suck it up and take it in stride. Routine becomes both their comfort and their cross. So why do so many people reach the end of their lives feeling empty, sensing that they somehow missed the meaning of it all?

I remember as a boy I found a board game at a local drugstore that was marked down from about four dollars to fifty cents! I opened the box, and all the pieces appeared to be intact, so I paid for the game with the fifty cents I'd earned mowing lawns. I ran home as fast as I could and made arrangements for a friend to come over and play the game with me.

The game was a war game called Guadalcanal, and as we were setting it up, I discovered that the directions or rules of play were missing. Undaunted, we played the game according to the rules and strategies we assumed were appropriate for a war game.

After playing the game literally all night and throughout the next day, we finally gave up because we had no idea how to win. We had all the pieces and gave it a lot of time, but the rules we used led nowhere.

My friend and I had wasted nearly two days of our precious summer vacation, but many of us waste a large chunk of our lives doing essentially the same thing. We may play with zeal, we may play with seeming purpose, but at some point most of us realize that our objectives and strategies don't lead to where we thought they would. We are engaged in the game, but we don't know how to win.

The Tale of Two Men

I grew up in a small town in eastern Oregon. When I was 12 years old, a young man in his twenties was killed instantly in an industrial accident. Just a few weeks earlier, on New Year's Eve, he was at church with his young wife and two small children. As the clock passed midnight, he joined everyone else at the front of the church to start the new year with prayer.

As the clock reached 12:15 AM that first day of January, people began to leave the altar and mingle as they left the church. But this man stayed at the front and prayed for some time all alone. On the way home his wife was talking about events in the upcoming year when Burt made the comment, "I won't be here." His wife looked at him and said, "What do you mean you won't be here, Burt?" He just looked at her and said, "I won't be here."

Burt told his wife that while he was praying, he believed God had told him he was going to die soon even though he was just in his mid-twenties and had no medical issues. Interestingly, just two months earlier Burt had purchased a life insurance policy following a somewhat spontaneous meeting. His wife felt that paying the premium would be a struggle, but they managed to make their first payment in the middle of December.

Around ten o'clock on January 4, Burt's supervisor at the lumbermill asked him to climb to the top of a large machine that had stopped working because the sudden extreme cold weather had caused some material inside to freeze together. Burt grabbed a long metal pole and climbed the side ladder, and then he started to jam the pole into the frozen material to break it up. As he raised the pole again in preparation to plunge it down, the top of the pole hit a high-voltage city power line, and Burt was killed instantly. The insurance company initially thought Burt committed suicide, but the investigation clearly showed that Burt was not suicidal, and no one could have planned this kind of accident.

His funeral was the very first funeral I attended. As I entered the packed church, I squeezed between two people on the back row and looked toward the front through a sea of shoulders. I instantly froze as I saw this man's pale, lifeless body lying slightly elevated above the edge of the half-opened casket at the front of the church. A wave of memories came rushing through my mind.

When I was in third grade, Burt had been my Sunday school teacher. While most men his age during the '60s were chasing girls and having fun, Burt spent his Saturday afternoons taking a handful of obnoxious eight-year-old boys to the park or sledding, and then he spent Sunday morning teaching us about what was important to him: his faith. As I looked at him in the casket, I remembered the Sunday nights at Shakey's Pizza parlor, the rides in his black 1934 Ford coupe, and flying down a snowy hill on a toboggan with his wife, Connie. He was dead, but he is still vividly alive in my mind 35 years later.

I recently read a newspaper story about another man, a 48-year-old guy named Edward who lived in New Hampshire. Edward was a likable guy who, together with his girlfriend, had two children. He got along well with people and was a frequent babysitter for friends and neighbors. The kids called him Uncle Buddha.

Unfortunately, Edward died from liver failure. He did not have proper identification when he was admitted to the hospital, so his fingerprints were submitted to authorities for analysis.

The police discovered that 17 years earlier, Edward had another family—complete with wife and children—and lived in Vermont. But Edward vanished when authorities charged him with sexually assaulting his daughter, and he eventually carved out a new life in the state next door. His new family and friends didn't know he was a fugitive. Even after 17 years and two kids, no one in New Hampshire seems to have actually known Edward.

Around the time of his funeral, Edward's two families met for the first time. A reporter asked Ed, Edward's 23-year-old namesake from his abandoned family, how they were all handling the shock of Edward's dual lives. He told the reporter, "Now that it's over, it's over. That's pretty much our take on it. But...it's just starting for them."

Ed continued, "He was a good person, but he had a dark side, and he hid it from these people."

Edward's two children in New Hampshire might spend years sifting through the ashes of their memories, trying to construct some realistic image of Edward. The two families could spend months struggling to answer the question, who was in that casket? Then again, after a few days or weeks, neither family—or anyone else—may give Edward much thought. When the image of a person is ruptured beyond repair, the idea that they ever lived sometimes evaporates.

As I read the article, my mind flashed back to the funeral 35 years earlier. Edward's story was in such contrast to Burt's story that I could not help but think of the many years of Edward's life that were suddenly meaningless. I realized that I still think about Burt and his influence on my life. His name is still spoken in the land of the living. But the truth erased Edward's life in an instant.

Edward probably did not choose to have his life end that way. In fact, the opposite is probably closer to the truth: Edward did not choose *not* to have his life end that way.

Reassessing the Future

Many of us give little thought to the end other than ensuring that we will have provided for the financial security of our loved ones and perhaps that we have, in some way, made peace with our Maker. Although these are important, the truth is that the things that will have the biggest impact on our loved ones cannot be left in a will. And making peace with God should release you to live life on a higher level now, not merely provide some sort of comfort as you gasp your last breath.

Perhaps that is why as some people get older they begin to question the direction and priorities of their lives. These people become unsure of who they really are, and they realize that most of the people closest to them don't really know them either. And in all honesty, they recognize that they don't really know the people they care the most about. When they see the gaping hole they are willing to risk what they spent most of their lives pursuing just for a chance to obtain a token of what they assigned little value to in the prime of their life.

We've all known both men and women who have amassed money, power, and prestige, only to set it aside to focus on their family. Robert Reich, former United States Secretary of Labor, left his position to spend time with his sons during their teenage years. Former senior presidential adviser Karen Hughes left her job to focus on her family relationships.

Although we often hear high-profile "relationships trump money and power" stories like these, abrupt life decisions aren't limited to the rich or powerful. People in your community might make decisions like that every day. A man of modest means works decades to set aside just enough money for retirement. But newspapers don't report his decision to spend it all in an attempt to reestablish a stunted relationship with a son or daughter.

Know Thyself

But this book is not about death, nor is it about decisions you make in your twilight years. It isn't just about relationships either. Rather, the chapters that follow are about life—about making sure that you really live before you die.

To use a computer software analogy, this book is about identifying a program that is—and has been—running undetected in your system your whole life. Although you probably don't see it on your "desktop," it affects the way both your hardware and software work. It is a program designed to lead you toward a certain objective, and its intent is to keep bringing you back toward your original design each time you get distracted by other endeavors and appetites.

Look down the road for a moment. Ask yourself these questions: If I continue the direction I'm heading right now, where will I end up in 10 years? In 20 years? Where am I going?

Or picture yourself on a shooting range. Before you squeeze the trigger, pull your head back from the scope of the rifle for just a moment and take a wider look. What have you been focusing on? Is that the right target for you?

You are not on this earth by accident. God was intentional when He made you. Your life has an internal sense of direction, and you can really live only if you embrace the person God made you to be. But as we will see, most of us aren't necessarily headed in the direction God wants us to go. Consequently, we will continue to be restless until we begin the journey back to who we really are. We must follow the ancient admonition to "know thyself."

The Invisible Man

Several years ago I realized my life was not going the way I wanted it to go. I didn't have a crisis in my life, and things weren't going badly. In fact, it was just the opposite. Things were going very well in my family life, business life, and academic studies. Yet in spite of this I was still unsettled—a little restless.

I had experienced the same feeling years before when the situation was just the opposite—things *were* going badly. At that time life felt futile on one hand and unexplored on the other. During those days I dreamed of the time when things would change for the better and I could experience the sense of satisfaction that seemed to elude me. Yet here I was in the good times, and both settledness and satisfaction remained at a distance. I had traveled through years of life only to find I was no closer to where I thought I wanted to be. Why?

Over the next year or so I was forced to wrestle with the whole idea of life and living. Why did I have an underlying sense of dissatisfaction—regardless of what I did? Was I just a malcontent, or was something missing? If something *was* missing, then that *something* was determined to harangue me.

It was almost as if the person God made me to be was somehow detached from the person I had become. Why? Where was the *real* me? What happened to sever him from who I had become?

At some point way back when, I think I may have begun to live a life of quiet expectations. What did the teachers expect? What did my parents expect? What did my boss expect? What did my pastor expect? What did my coworkers expect? I'm not talking about assignments, chores, tasks, or promises. Those are easy—they are stated.

No, I'm talking about the unstated expectations—the kind you don't recognize until you sense you may have violated them. Or, the ones you put on yourself simply because you feel you *should* be a certain way, or do a certain thing. Some men recoil when they sense other people's expectations. Other men put them on like a coat when they sense people perceive qualities they know inside they do not have. We either chase them or run from them. But whether we embrace or recoil from expectations, they end up changing us.

I began to sense that the real me was on the edge of disappearing altogether. I spent enormous time and effort trying to become the person I thought I needed to be—at the time. Father. Husband. Scholar. Executive. Christian. Each one felt like a role I played in a particular situation. But if my life was measured by who I was in one of these situations—or by who I needed to be in any of these situations—then perhaps my life as a whole had lost its meaning.

Was Marcus Ryan a person? Or was he just playing varying roles, like the '70s sitcom actor? At that man's funeral people imitated characters from the roles he played and mimicked the lines he delivered. But who *was* he? If I were to die right then, would anyone at my funeral who knew me from a segment or role I played recognize the whole man?

Could the man God made me to be fade away, somehow replaced by a caricature? Would the real me pass into eternity never having matured, while the imitation me staggers restlessly across the earth for decades?

Many people believe life is a test, meant to determine our fitness for the next world. I don't. I think life is a journey during which we begin to live in eternity and influence certain others around us to do the same. The alternative is either to try to hit moving targets, to build a statue of the person we think we should be, or never to give any serious consideration to the destination—to the man who will lie in the casket at the end of his days.

I had to find and embrace the man God made me to be regardless of who that man was. That man must live before I will die, or I would never have really lived. I may have made money, earned academic degrees, sired children, and attained a modicum of power. But all of these would mean little unless they were directly related to the man God made. By themselves they would only have momentary meaning. However, if they *are* part of that man, then all those things—money, degrees, power—would have meaning and value as contributions to the process of becoming a vessel of honor.

But how could I do that? I didn't even know where to begin looking. As I discussed this struggle with my wife and a couple of close friends I sensed that they saw in me things I hadn't seen. I began to suspect that they could be valuable in the process of recovering my true identity. To know myself, I had to allow myself to be known—by certain other people and by God. My desire to engage life and recapture my purpose would necessarily include a quest to be known.

I believe the same may be true for you. Whether you realize it or not, your entire life is driven by one thing: To be known. The only motivation even close to it is to know someone else. All other drives and motives such as money, fame, and even sex are mere means to this end. Your life will be complete and meaningful or unfulfilled and pointless based on the degree to which you "know thyself," to which you are uniquely known, and to which you uniquely know others.

Undiagnosed Symptoms

Life is a quest to be known?

A few men I've talked with said they hadn't given life's purpose much thought. But these same men readily admitted they sensed that something wasn't right in their life. And although they didn't know what it was, they felt that they were getting farther and farther off a course they couldn't seem to find.

Other men spoke of a feeling of restlessness. This was certainly true for those who were going through changes such as a divorce, job issues, and problems with children. But the restlessness was just as common in men with an established routine. Sometimes these men expressed it as an unsettledness— an uneasy feeling. Is restlessness just part of the male baggage?

Or is the restlessness a symptom of something else? On the good side, restlessness keeps us in the fight—it forces us to continue to struggle. It reminds us that something isn't right. Unfortunately, too many men ignore the restlessness and settle for futility.

A large, silent group of men are convinced that their family would be better off without them. A pastor in California recently told me that he had two calls the previous week from men who confided that exact feeling to him. They both independently said, "Pastor, I just feel my family would be better off financially, emotionally—in pretty much every way—if I weren't here." The pastor knew "if I weren't here" meant "if I were dead." He said that this wasn't the only time he'd heard these words. In fact, he hears them all the time, and each man who shares these feelings thinks he is the only one who feels that way.

Would your wife and kids exchange you for enough money to solve their current financial problems? Do you ever feel the people around you would be better off if you just quietly stepped away? I have stopped being amazed at the number of men who feel this way, or who feel restless or off course. But what *does* still amaze me is how men can hide their feelings so effectively behind their words and appearance. How can feelings so widespread, so pervasive, and so destructive lie just beneath the surface of so many men, and yet go undetected by their friends and family?

The Center of Your Being

Distilled to their essence, the feelings of restlessness, unsettledness, uneasiness, and inadequacy—and others such as futility, despair, and worthlessness—come from a sense of being "unknown," both by yourself and by others.

I was on the telephone with a new acquaintance when the subject of this book came up. The man I was speaking with had been very successful in real estate and other ventures, and he was also known for his strong personal faith. He told me that for many years people had asked if he had a favorite Bible verse. He candidly responded that he really didn't.

Then one day on a business trip to Louisiana he was reading the Bible and came across the phrase "to be known." He said, "I felt as if something had touched a nerve deep in my heart. I had no idea that there was a desire more intense than love, success, or even a strong faith." He instantly realized there was a need at the very core of his life that he had to somehow understand because, in retrospect, he could see how it drove every other desire and motive.

The new Segway Human Transporter is a fascinating invention, a form of personal transportation that moves when it senses subtle shifts in the rider's body weight. The user holds on to handles as he stands on a platform with two big wheels. He then accelerates or slows down by gently leaning forward or backward. The cycle's forward motion and ability to keep itself and the rider upright are both handled by a high-tech gyroscope.

The gyroscope gives the cycle its direction and stability, and it sets the Segway apart from any other type of personal transportation. You can't move a Segway by pushing buttons or even by using your legs to push it like you would an old-fashioned scooter. You have to trust yourself to the function of the gyroscope.

A similar devise is at the core of your being. It is a spiritual gyroscope, and its purpose is to move you down the path of being known. When you realize it is there, and if you will trust it, it will keep you balanced and move you forward. You can pursue success, physical pleasure, or extreme sports and not necessarily move forward. You may spin in place, and that feeling might be exhilarating. But at the end of the day, at the end of your life, you will realize you went nowhere. You missed the mark.

Why? Because that is how you are made. As you will discover in the next chapters, that core need to be known for who you really are is what makes you different from animals in this life, and it relates to what happens after death.

The River of Life

When I was young, I went stream fishing with my father. He was an aggressive fisherman, and I was a daydreamer. He would wade the deep water, move down the stream from rock to rock, and sometimes push through thick brush on the bank of the river. This went on for miles.

I would lag behind, eventually laying aside my fishing pole in favor of skipping rocks across the water. I would find a handful of flat rocks along the bank of the river and side-arm them one at a time, skipping them along the surface. The objective was to make the most skips across the surface before the rock either sank or landed on the other side.

These two activities portray two approaches to life. Many people are just like me skipping rocks. Their life objective is to traverse the surface of living, making as many splashes as possible before ending up safely on the other side of life, safe and secure in the afterlife. They then look back on how many splashes they made and how cool they looked, and they are elated that they didn't end up sinking somewhere along the way.

But what if more of us lived the way my father fished the south fork of the Sprague River? He knew the area, but each time he walked the river, he explored new holes and revisited older ones. He discovered and rediscovered the river. He expected change, but he also renewed his knowledge of the river by going deeper, dealing with thick brush, and spending time to reach the hard-to-get-to places. He knew the river and the river seemed to know him. He was comfortable with the fact that he had to tease the fish out of the river each time he went.

Reflection

I am convinced that if you will commit to going deeper into understanding yourself, if you will allow God to push back the thick brush surrounding the places you've hidden from yourself and others, and if you will trust that God has a path for your life, you will hit the target. At the end you can only look back. Today you can look forward. Then, the end will be what it is. Now, the end will be what you make it. You can still adjust your aim before you squeeze the trigger.

You do not have to end your life alone. Six men who truly know you can put their shoulder to the weight of your casket and stand as witnesses to your life. You can leave this world and enter a place where you know, even as you are known. Instead of hearing, "I never knew you; depart from me," you can hear God summon you by name. You can hear His voice joyfully exclaim, "My son...I take great pride in who you are. Come home! Enter into your rest."

Just as importantly, you can better understand how to live here and now. And as you'll see in the next chapter, that understanding will come as you engage a very special quest.

2

THE QUEST

Everybody must learn this lesson somewhere—
that it costs something to be what you are.
SHIRLEY ABBOTT

....

IN THE LATE 1990S, a sheep dog traveled about four miles to find his previous owner after being moved to a new home. The collie had been with an elderly man named Denis since he was a pup, and the bond between the two was very tight. Denis named his dog Duke.

Five months before Duke returned to Denis he had been placed with another family. But in the days leading up to Christmas he ran off and made his way across busy roads and around heavy traffic on his way to the old man.

Many pet owners have shared stories of animals traveling much farther than four miles to return home. Dogs have traveled hundreds, even thousands of miles through foul weather and across rough terrain.

This story is unique because the dog didn't go home. Instead, the dog found Denis' grave at Saint James' Parish Church, even though he had not been shown where Denis was buried the previous summer. Police found Duke curled up and whimpering atop Denis' grave on Christmas Eve. Sheila, the dog's new owner, said, "I don't think there is any doubt Duke was on a mission. It was just something he had to do."

The Nature of a Quest

Duke could stay where he was no longer. It wasn't as though he had been ignored or mistreated. Denis' widow had been diligent in finding a good home for the dog. Yet for some reason he was compelled to leave. You would think that Duke would go back to the place where he lived with Denis for so many years. But he wasn't looking for a place. He wasn't looking for security. He wanted something more, and it couldn't be found in his new home. It couldn't be found where he used to live. It might never be found, but something deep inside told him he had to try. That is the nature of a quest.

A quest is a unique journey. You don't find too many people moving from quest to quest, partly because a quest is usually something formidable and daunting. To further complicate things, true quests are hard to recognize.

A quest isn't discovered in a brainstorming session. It isn't something you wake up in the morning and add to your task list, like "start on a quest today."

A quest is also more than a goal. A person sets a goal assuming it is attainable, but a quest is forbidding, and the prospect of failure is very real. It most often begins with an epiphany or a sudden realization, as if a person receives an edict. Quests can seem elusive, almost mysterious—so much so that they make great fodder for movies.

Frodo the Hobbit took on a seemingly impossible quest in the J.R.R. Tolkien trilogy, The Lord of the Rings. An unlikely character, he began a quest he didn't choose but rather accepted. And although he knew the goal—to return the ring to the molten fire, where it was forged—he couldn't begin to comprehend the path. He had no idea of the obstacles, the length of the journey, the need for help from stranger and friend, or even the certainty of betrayal. The thing he was probably most certain of was the likelihood of failure. Frodo reluctantly started on a quest he little understood but was compelled to pursue, and it changed him—and those around him—forever.

Whether you know it or not, you too are on a quest. The core of this quest is so deeply ingrained in your being that you can't separate it from who you are. It is the elephant in the room of your heart...so visible that it is invisible. This quest is not for glory and not for riches. It is much more subtle and elusive than that. It is a quest to be known.

Life Can Make Sense

Many men react against the idea of a quest to be known. As a friend of mine said, "I'm *afraid* of being known. I don't want to be discovered and exposed as a fraud, a lesser man than people perceive me to be."

Can you relate to his feelings? I can. But as you will see, being known is not about being exposed. It has little to do with baring your soul to other people. Instead, it is about the pathway to self-discovery. It is a mechanism that protects your identity and refreshes that image when it comes under the particularly savage attacks of the workplace. The path to being known unlocks the prison of the fear of being discovered, while at the same time giving you access to your own unique talents and destiny.

If you truly understand that you are on a quest to be known—and that others are on the same quest—your relationships will be richer, your goals will come into focus, and your personal level of satisfaction will rise significantly. Things will just make more sense. Your ability to evaluate and determine a course of action will feel instinctive, whereas before it seemed awkward. This subtle shift will allow life to come to you rather than you muscling your way through it. Let me give you an example.

A Subtle Shift

When I was 18 years old, I worked in a lumber mill on what was called the dry chain. It consisted of a series of parallel chains with links about three inches wide that carried dry lumber from the planer—where the rough wood had been smoothed on the tops and sides—out to where it would be stacked. Think of it as a big conveyor belt moving lumber that is lying sideways across the belt with the end sticking out on one side.

I was one of five or six men who would stand on a platform next to the chains and move a specific size and grade of lumber to a stack on the ground below. This was done by putting my weight on the board so that the end closest to me made contact with a four-inch round steel roller that spun as it carried the wood from the chains down to the ground. I would keep my weight on it until the end of the board reached my hands, at which time I would grab the end and let the momentum of the board carry it out to where I could drop it into place. This entire process took less than three seconds per board.

When I started the job I had the same problem everyone else had learning the craft. I tried to muscle the board off the chain and feed it onto the stack. The problem with this approach was twofold: I carried the full weight of each board from the chain until it landed below. And rather than taking three seconds, this approach took about fifteen to twenty seconds per board. The chain constantly stopped to allow me to catch up. Additionally, the board seldom made it in place, and I was physically exhausted after about an hour.

Every man who was hired to "pull chain" started with the assumption that he could pick it up in a matter of minutes or at the most within a few hours. But a new chainman usually took about two weeks to figure out how to let the board do the work. The amazing thing was that a very subtle shift in method did the trick, and the shift typically happened very quickly. One minute you were exhausted and everyone around you was paying the price for your ignorance, and the next you were swiftly and instinctively laying the boards down with very little effort.

Men typically muscle through life. We bear the weight of each board by ourselves, seldom realizing how much this affects others. No wonder we are exhausted. But the real pain comes in realizing that the people around us are the ones who pay the price. So we grimace. We suck it up. We go on. And once again the chains of life are stopped and everyone gets to help clean up our mess.

When you truly grasp the subtle truth that a significant drive in men is to be known, you will enjoy an instinctive approach to life. You'll just *know* things. And not just you—your understanding of a man's quest to be known will affect the lives of the people around you. It will change you as a husband, a father, an employer or employee, and a friend.

Jettison the Assumptions

Admittedly, the idea that you are on a quest to be known can seem abstract, vague, or tough to get your arms around. It also flies in the face of cultural assumptions about the nature of men, including these:

1. Men are loners.
2. Men are hunters.

3. Men want to be known only by reputation.

4. Men are not relational.

5. For men, being known is the same thing as having a group of men you hang with, like your golfing buddies.

6. A man needs to be in an accountability group.

If you are to consider the possibility that you are on a quest to be known, then you have to go beyond assumptions and wrestle with this concept. It may require you to spend time and dig a little deeper into those subtle, powerful forces that drive you, even though they may seem vague and ethereal. These forces can seldom be understood in a simple and formulaic "ten steps" or "seven secrets" style, yet they influence everything you do. The deceptive thing is that they are so obvious you can't see them. You seldom consciously recognize their power until something happens that causes them to break in on your life in an obvious way, effecting significant change.

The Power of the Intangible

Most of the time men live their lives focused on a goal or an outcome. We concentrate on tangible accomplishments such as getting a specific job or promotion, buying a house in a certain neighborhood, or perhaps winning a racing title or football championship. We set financial, vocational, and fitness goals, and we chart a path to their completion. We like to do things that require a checklist, even if the list is simply in our heads—things we can physically or mentally scratch off as we complete them. Little by little, and through a lot of work and sacrifice, we fulfill our dreams and reach our goals.

But what about the man who was thriving as he followed his dreams and goals and suddenly and abruptly changed his course? What could possibly cause a man who spent years setting and achieving goal after goal to abandon his list?

In 2001, Pat Tillman was well into a successful career as a professional football player. To achieve that level of success in a very competitive business, a person must be not only talented but also focused, disciplined, and committed to his goals. But Pat turned his back on a $3.6 million contract with the NFL Arizona Cardinals—unexpectedly quitting the thing he spent his life preparing for—and joined the United States Army. Was he motivated by his love for freedom? Patriotism? Dave McGinnis, Tillman's former coach with the Cardinals, told MSNBC News, "Pat knew his purpose in life. He proudly walked away from a career in football to a greater calling."

Several months ago I read about a middle-aged executive who had been very successful in business. His wife of many years was dead, and all of his children were out of the home. He had accumulated a fairly substantial amount of money over the years, so he was in the position to comfortably retire early. He was not facing any crises, and he seemed to enjoy life very much.

One day he called his kids together, gave each one a sum of money, and told them that he had given the rest of his estate to charity. He then informed them that he was becoming a monk. He made a vow of poverty and chose to live the remainder of his life in service to others. Was this change the result of his faith? Was it a sense of duty? A search for peace? Or something else?

Whatever the force behind the dramatic changes in the lives of these two men, the goals and dreams they developed and pursued for the better part of their lives were supplanted. They were compelled by a force that was indiscernible by many, but one that reprioritized their entire worlds.

Freedom, patriotism, peace, faith, and even love are all hard to define. Ask three people to define love, and you will get four different answers. The same thing will happen when you try to define freedom—even faith and respect. But could anyone believe that because they are hard to precisely define they don't significantly affect decisions and choices people make? If we really think about it, these concepts shape the tangible goals and dreams we make and pursue day after day.

None more so than your need to be known for who you really are. In fact, the need to be known shapes and influences many of these other concepts. For instance, when love is boiled down to its essence, it is intricately linked to knowing and being known. We see this in 1 Corinthians 13—the love chapter.

After describing love's characteristics and its supremacy, the apostle Paul wrote, "Now we see [perceive or know] in a mirror dimly, but then face to face." Then, as if to be sure we really get what he's saying, he repeats that concept using different words, "Now I know in part: then I shall know fully, even as I have been fully known." Paul seems certain that we are all on a journey to being fully known.

Being Known

Being known is not about being a celebrity or the life of the party. Frankly, most men are not that way. Being known isn't about everyone knowing you or about being vulnerable to a bunch of strangers or Sunday acquaintances.

Being known is multifaceted. You discover yourself and your unique qualities through interaction with others. But also, the other people serve as witnesses to your life. They are the keepers of your story. Just to make a point, let me say this: If you don't exist in anyone's memory, if no one knew you or remembers you, did you really exist?

Quite some time ago I was invited to attend a small gathering of what I was told would be the future leaders of evangelical Christianity in the United States. The invitation flattered and surprised me. When the time came, I flew to the designated city and joined the small group of men in a banquet room. I am always a bit awkward at small talk, but I engaged a few people in conversation and involved myself in the night's agenda.

A few months after the event I was backstage with my wife at a function associated with her work. Several of the men who organized and hosted the previous event were there as well, and because only a few of us were in the room we all began to converse. As we talked, these men described how fantastic the previous event—the one I had attended—had been. A good deal of the time these men spoke directly to me, and I soon realized by the way they talked that they had no idea I had attended the same event.

The original group had been small, and attendance was by invitation only. They hosted it. But in their mind, I was never there. They had prayed with me, and we had eaten meals together. We had talked *mano a mano*. Yet I didn't exist.

Although the situation was amusing, it was also sobering. I wasn't insulted. Instead, I had a new appreciation for the value of my friendships with the half dozen or so men I have come to regard as friends. They know me. They know I exist.

A Few Good Men

The last part of the concept of being known is that you also want to know others uniquely, and you innately want to help others discover themselves. You possess the power to help others define themselves, and they you. This power can be abused, but it was intended for good.

Because of the potential in these relationships, they are rarely and carefully entered. They develop over time. They are uncommon and are seldom slap-on-the-back, "let's hang out" friendships. Those are fine and serve a purpose but are not as uniquely powerful as the relationships in which you help others know their true selves, and they you.

In a nutshell, you want other people—a few good men, your wife, your children—to know your story uniquely. Though they will each know you in many of the same ways, each one will know something about you the others don't know. Only together can they fully understand you. Ultimately, at the end of your life, you want your family to walk behind the six men who carry your casket and, one by one, tell your story and celebrate your life.

As my father reclined on the hospital-style bed in his bedroom during the last few days of his life, he told us stories of his life. He talked about being raised by his stepfather in Vermont after his mother left for the big city. He talked about his time in the military and becoming a Christian. He told us all kinds of stories of his work, his disappointments, and his dreams. He talked about the unique qualities he saw in each of his children and grandchildren.

In those last few days, my father was compelled to retell us his story. He wanted to be sure we knew him. My children were just babies then, so I tell his story now. I tell my children who their grandfather was. His story is part of our story. He extended himself into the future because his story is integrated with ours, and we can't tell our story without knowing his.

Specificity in Being Known

You've probably noticed that when I write about being known I often use the words *unique* and *certain*. I use these words because God created Adam specifically and uniquely, distinct from other creatures. When Adam named the other creatures, he could find none like himself, none that would be a suitable partner. None like him. Adam was a unique being looking for a particular helper. He wasn't looking for anyone. He was looking for someone.

You too are looking for people who are like you, yet who are also distinct from you. People to whom you can give the name *friend* or *wife*. You want to know them better and differently—more intimately—than others do. And you want them to know you—to understand and perceive you for who you are.

The Weight of Mischaracterization

Did you ever begin to reveal yourself to someone, only to have him reject you once you began to disclose the real you? How about the opposite? Has someone dismissed you because he misjudged you? When others form the wrong impression of you or put you in a box, you feel—at the least—unnerved and unsettled. You may seethe and fume under the surface. Your confidence may be shaken, and you might question whether or not you even know yourself.

Sometimes the opposite is true. People see you as someone you know you aren't. They may perceive you as a committed family man or dedicated Christian. Maybe they see you as a man of character, but you think of all the times no one saw what you were doing or knew what you were thinking. You then find yourself trying to reinforce the positive perception others have of you, all the while thinking, *If they only knew.* And so the struggle between being the person people see you as on one hand and altering the misconception others have of you on the other becomes a nagging source of discontent. In Luke's Gospel, Jesus told a parable about people trapped on each side of the equation. In our day it might have sounded something like this:

Two men went to church to pray. The first man was a law professor and was held in high regard by everyone. He was very comfortable in his place of leadership in the church and was visibly charitable and culturally refined. His prayer was a prayer of gratitude that he was a man of character and class—blameless, or so he wanted God and everyone else to think. He was careful to point out that he was not like the man seated at the back of the church. Everyone could count on that. The professor had a reputation to keep up.

The man at the back of the church entered after everyone else was already in place and after the service had begun. He squeezed between the closed back doors and sat on the last row, wrapped in an oversized winter coat. He hunched down, hoping that no one would recognize him. They probably wouldn't have if the professor had not pointed him out.

The man at the back ran an investment firm that had been in the local newspapers for months. Some people whispered that he ran a Ponzi scheme, while others thought he was involved in some kind of stock fraud. The man was wealthy. Like the law professor, he too was well-known. But in his case, that wasn't a good thing.

He wasn't sure why he risked ridicule by coming to church, but at that moment he had more pressing matters. With the collar of his coat turned up around his face, he knelt on the floor and half-laid on the back of the bench in front of him. With deep groans that were audible but not discernible, the man prayed to God for mercy. This man had a reputation to live down.

Many of us are where these two men were. The professor was trying to maintain his persona, the image others had of him. He had a reputation to maintain. The investment banker was trying to distance himself from people's perception. He had a reputation to repair.

A gentleman at my church recently elaborated on this Scripture one Sunday morning. He said that he used to speak at conferences quite a bit, and he admitted to having a deep fear that at some conference a person would stand up in the back and say, "Hey, wait a minute. I know who you are. You're the guy who used to do thus and so." The man even began to wake up at night, dreading the next event for fear that someone would confront him when he spoke.

The Person You Want to Be

In addition to the unsettledness of being mischaracterized and the fear of being found out, sometimes as we get older something happens to jar us into realizing that who we have become is not the person we thought we would be. Let me ask you a question. Are you the person today that you thought you'd be at this age? Don't let money or status determine your answer. Are you the father, the husband, the friend, or the man of faith you thought you would be when as a kid you imagined the person you would become?

I was listening to the XM satellite radio '70s channel one day while driving down I-64 in Virginia. A song came on that suddenly transported my mind back to a time when I was 18 years old and cruising on South Sixth Street in Klamath Falls, Oregon. For some reason the music brought back vivid memories, and I felt as if I were in the car 30 years ago, thinking the thoughts I thought then.

The memories provided a rich picture of how I imagined myself to be at my age now. I remembered the traits I assumed I would have. I recalled how certain I was that I would have worked out my quirks. I thought of the image I had of me as a father, a husband, and a faithful Christian. As I compared the picture of who I thought I'd be with who I'd become, I found I was disappointed in many ways.

As I considered those two images over a period of months, I began to see the person I really wanted to be, but for some reason I was detached from him. He was the person I always thought I would become, but he stood apart from me. I remembered a song Tim Hosman wrote that didn't make as much sense to me when I heard it in the early 1980s as it does now:

> There's a person that I really want to be
> But he's trapped and buried deep inside of me
> Though he kicks for life and fights for air to breathe
> He's the person that I really want to be
>
> Don't know how he's lived so long inside my soul
> For the winter months down there can be so cold
> Guess his will to survive has not grown old
> He's the person that I wish was in control
>
> But he gets buried by the sands of time
> Waiting patiently to be a friend of mine
> And through the passing years I guess that I've grown blind
> And it seems to me his face is growing dim
> But I really wish that I were him

I have good news. There is a reason you feel alienated from the person you really want to be. There is a reason you grow weary under the weight of wearing a mask of your own making or that others have placed on you. There is a reason you become frustrated and unnerved when you are mischaracterized. It is because your entire being absolutely and categorically rejects being unknown. It wants you to wake up and recognize that to experience a deep sense of fulfillment, you must make the journey toward being known for who you really are.

Why? Because God made you this way. Like Duke, you must set out on a journey to return to a place you've never been. Remember, you do not choose this quest. You accept it.

Believe the Story

The day after Christmas in 2004, a 9.0 earthquake rocked the Indian Ocean and set off a tsunami that killed hundreds of thousands of people on three continents. Some people in the tsunami's path felt the quake, but most did not. They had no idea that 100-foot waves were bearing down on them.

As the quake pulled the seas back from the shorelines, fascinated tourists watched fish flop and sea life struggle to find the water that had suddenly vanished. People explored the naked ocean floor and chatted about the adventure until it was too late to move to safety.

The island of Simeulue, home to 75,000 people, was just 40 miles from the quake's epicenter. According to the Associated Press, though the residents felt quakes before, they had never seen a tsunami. But as the violent quake subsided and residents regained their footing, they saw the water move quickly out and away from the beach. And they ran like the wind.

One man threw his two small, startled children into a wheelbarrow and pushed it as fast as he could up the foothills and into the mountain. His children asked no questions because their father clearly knew exactly what he was doing.

Why did the father make such a swift and instinctive response? This is why: When he was a child, he had heard the story of the mighty waves. His grandparents passed it on to his parents, and his parents passed it on to him. The details varied a little here and there, but the message didn't: If you ever feel an earthquake and see the water peel away from the shore, don't wait, don't watch, don't think—just run. Run as fast as you can up and into the mountains. So that is exactly what he did—and all 75,000 residents on the island.

Nothing like this had ever happened in his life or his parents'. No one had organized civil emergency drills, created a PowerPoint presentation with an animated tsunami, or fastidiously explained tectonic plates. But he had heard the story, and he believed it—and he ran.

Just 30 minutes after the quake, the first wave hit the little island and destroyed absolutely everything along the coastline. Homes and businesses disappeared. With little more than the shirts on their backs, the islanders looked down on the ravaged coastline. Most of what had defined their lives an hour before was now gone.

When it was all over, one side of the island had sunk 11 inches into the sea, and the other side jutted four feet above the previous water line. The island was decimated. But the man and his family lived. In fact, of the 75,000 people who lived on the island, just seven died. The islanders believed the story.

In the next chapter I will tell you a story about the origin of your quest to be known.

3

THE SOURCE

You wouldn't be so thirsty if you had never tasted water.
BISHOP FULTON SHEEN

....

I WAS IN HIGH SCHOOL WHEN the movie *American Graffiti* was released. It generated quite a buzz and was quickly followed by the TV series *Happy Days*. Both had an immediate transforming effect on the two parallel streets that formed a small loop through the downtown streets of my hometown. The loop that had once been abandoned on Friday and Saturday nights was suddenly filled with carloads of teenagers, honking horns and hanging out of car windows as they "dragged Main Street."

My friends and I poured the money from our part-time jobs into cars and car parts. Chrome wheels and loud glass pack mufflers were a must. I had an orange '67 Camero with a big white racing stripe running down the middle, just like the one on the cover of a model car kit. My Camero was made to drag Main, sound great, and get the girls' attention.

Most of us hit the downtown area after the high school game, and by ten o'clock the streets were packed and noisy. Traffic crawled. We commonly sat through five or six rotations of the traffic light just to move a single block.

Once in a while I was fortunate enough to be one of two cars at the front of the two-lane, one-way street waiting side by side for the light to turn green. This signaled my turn to rev the engine and burn the tires a bit, trying to provoke the car next to me into a race when the red light turned green. It wasn't much of a race. If you were lucky you had about 30 feet or so between the "starting line" and the bumper of the car stopped in the next block.

My friend Rich was already out of high school, so his full-time job gave him a lot more money to plow into his car. It was a Mustang with a modified big-block engine, and he was obsessed with building the fastest car. He transformed his Mustang into an incredible racing machine.

On the few occasions Rich took his car downtown it stalled every 30 seconds or so because it had a difficult time idling. This was not because of an engine problem, but because his Mustang was made to get to very high speeds very quickly—not move inches a minute. For months we begged him to give in and take his car downtown, and then in about 30 minutes it would overheat, forcing Rich to nurse it home.

That Mustang was not made for dragging Main Street. But what a difference when he took it out to an isolated section of highway just out of town called Orendale Draw. He was enormously successful. The car never stalled. It never overheated. It blew the doors off anything that came to that lonely stretch of road to race.

The funny thing was that Rich's car looked pretty much the same as every other car dragging Main Street. It didn't look like an Indy car or modified stock car. In fact, hardly anyone could notice a significant difference between his car and the other Mustangs downtown. But the car's appearance wasn't what made it so out of place and unsuccessful downtown. The difference was under the hood, in the transmission, and deep within the differential. The difference was what powered it. What drove it.

What's Under Your Hood?

Just as Rich's Mustang looked like the other cars on Main Street, mankind and animals share many similarities. Like man, much of what an animal does throughout its life serves one purpose: to stay alive. Like us, they eat, secure lodging, have sex, and even jockey for power. These things consume pretty much all the time animals have, and they take up a considerable amount of our time and effort. Building a home, protecting your family, and providing the essentials are necessary and worthwhile endeavors. In these ways, we are very much like the animals.

If we indeed are so much like animals, are we really any different? Yes, in one very important way. Have you ever heard of an animal committing suicide because of the futility of life?

Man recognizes that he exists. He knows he is alive, and he seeks some purpose for his existence. This capacity for self-examination and the accompanying need for meaning came from the same fundamental yet profound component of our nature.

Much of the world's population believes that man has a spiritual dimension, which Christians and others believe was "breathed" into him by his Maker. The Scriptures say that God breathed into man the breath of life, and he became a "living being." Does that mean that animals are not living beings, or does that term have a greater meaning?

Scripture uses two Hebrew words to describe the animals created on the fifth day, those created on the sixth day, and man. These two words are used each time, and they are usually translated "living creature." But a very slight variation the third time the words are used points to a creation that is similar yet distinct from the other living creatures. This implication that man has some attribute that makes him unique from all animals, combined with the reference to man being made in God's image, shifts the focus away from dissimilarities with animals to similarities with God.

People generally acknowledge that God is Spirit, not matter. Therefore, the natural conclusion is that what God breathed into man—the distinct difference in this creation that separates man from other living creatures, and the aspect of mankind that is made in God's image—is man's spiritual nature. We are living creatures and we are spiritual beings, which makes us "living beings."

This puts us in a unique and perhaps uncomfortable position. Just like all creation, we are made by God, and we live on this earth as God's creation. But unlike the world around us, we are uniquely spiritual. We live somewhere between our physical needs and our spiritual desire.

Your Unique Characteristics

We know our physical needs drive much of our activity, but because we are equally spiritual we must ask, what does the spiritual side of us seek; what is its desire? We begin to answer these questions by considering what a spiritual being is.

Eternal

The first characteristic of man's spirituality is that it is eternal. You sense in your heart that something happens after death, that some part of you will live past the grave.

The earliest records of man, painted on the walls of caves, tell stories of what our ancestors thought would happen in the next life. Even ancient grave sites reveal a belief in life after death because the dead are surrounded by personal objects thought to be useful in the afterlife. As far back as records go humans have felt eternity in their hearts, and they recognized death as a door to the other side.

When my daughter was in the fifth grade we bought her a canary for her birthday. Everything was fine until one day when she came home from school and found the bird lying dead in the bottom of the cage. I wrapped the bird in tissue, put it in an old shoebox from my closet, and buried it in the backyard. We didn't pack any birdseed or bird toys in the box. We were sorry the bird had died, and we missed its companionship, but we didn't think we might see it again "on the other side."

Think about the last time you buried a family pet. Did you seriously ponder birdie heaven or hamster hell? Yet when a close friend or family member dies, you naturally think about what happens after death. You become acutely aware of a dimension of reality different from the here and now.

Creative

Another element of our spirituality is our creativity. We inherited from God the innate desire to create, to improve, and to perfect. This is different from the utilitarian drive inherent in all animals to produce shelter and food. You and I want to create and perfect simply for the sake of creating and perfecting. We want to see ourselves in what we create, and at the end of the day we want to look at what we've done and say, "It is good."

Genesis 2 says that God had not caused the desolate places to flourish because no man was available to work the ground, no one to take what happens naturally and groom it, no one to shape it in a way that would bring out its best. But then God made Adam and said, "Just do it!" What a great job.

A good friend of mine named Jeff is an administrator extraordinaire. He listens to the desires of the president of his organization and then focuses the staff in a way that both brings out their creative potential and fleshes out the administration's goals. I think he has an enormous sense of purpose when the people he works for and those who work with him look at what they accomplished and say, "Hey, that is good!"

Not Good

Books like *The Purpose-Driven Life* ring true because they touch an element of our spiritual nature and cause it to rise above animal instincts. They put a name to something we sense. We are purpose driven.

Others, such as *Wild at Heart,* play to the animal side. God mandated that mankind subdue, cultivate, and take responsibility for the earth. The created nature that is still very much a part of who we are is fused with a spirit, a purpose, and a focus, and we rise to the challenge like a wolf rises to the chase.

Although the tasks and challenges of the Garden engaged the eternal and creative aspects of man's spiritual nature, man needed more. God looked at man—a man individually armed with God's expressed purpose—and said, "Oh, this is not good." What? The rest of creation was good. How could something God created, equipped, and challenged not be good?

More fully stated, God looked at Adam and said, "It is not good that the man should be alone; I will make him a helper fit for him." Did God say this because Adam needed a female in order to procreate, to continue the line of mankind? Yes, but God's intent goes beyond the male-female combination required to produce children. If all man needed was the ability to have offspring, God could have used the phrase He used to recognize reproduction in all other living creatures, which was "according to its kind."

No, Adam needed a helper who corresponded to his nature. And as the verse goes on to say, God brought all the animals to Adam one by one to see what he would name them. But the Scripture seems to indicate that Adam did not see himself in any creature enough to cause him to name it in a way that corresponded to who he was. He had purpose. He had a challenge. But the spiritual nature that distinguished him from other creatures required even more. It required a relationship—a context for knowing another person and being known. In fact, this characteristic empowers the other aspects of his nature. Here's an illustration.

In the beginning of the 2005 CBS reality show *Survivor*, two tribes faced a reward challenge. The tribes had roughly divided into the age-wisdom tribe and the youth-strength tribe. The challenge was to be the first tribe to have all its members maneuver a land obstacle course, jump into a boat, and cross the finish line together.

But between the obstacle course and the boat race were large, heavy water cans and trunks filled with supplies, with each weighted with sand. Some trunks contained food, such as rice, and others contained a fire-making kit. The supplies were tied up with multiple ropes, so each one had to be untangled to be taken.

The obvious strategy was to get as many of the supplies as possible, but that strategy had to be balanced against the condition that only the team that won got to keep the supplies. So even if you were able to muscle the trunks and cans across the sand, through the jungle, and into the boats, they would be of no use if you couldn't be the first team to maneuver the heavy supplies and your eight team members across the water to the finish line.

The young, strong "Turks" used muscle and will to release the water and food and to drag them toward the boat, but in the process they inadvertently left the flint kit behind. The older team moved through the obstacle course and grabbed only the fire kit. They then moved as fast as possible to the boat and toward the finish line. Though the younger team was noticeably stronger and quicker, the older team's strategy worked, and they won the race and the reward.

The older team's strategy was simple enough. The food, water, and fire were all important. But with the fire, they could cook fish and other potential food around the beach and boil water to drink.

The younger team used considerable time and energy to release and move the water and food. If they had crossed the finish line first, their victory would have lasted only as long as the water. The rice was pretty much useless without the fire to cook it. Additionally, neither water nor bags of rice provide warmth or light at night. Fire made the rice useful, the water supply endless, the nights warmer, and the path clearer.

So while your eternal spiritual nature needs purpose, needs to be creative, and requires the ability to produce offspring, it needs something more.

The Story

I believe that the key insight into your spiritual nature is its quest to be known. It is the fire-making kit of your spiritual nature. And although it is not immediately discernible in the creation story, this core component of your spirituality is embedded in the text, "[God] breathed into his nostrils the breath of life; and man became a living being."

In the book *The Science of God*, Gerald Schroeder explores another translation of this verse that helped me understand how God set man apart from the rest of creation. In an Arabic translation of the Hebrew text, that verse reads more like this: "The Eternal God formed the adam dust from the ground and breathed into his nostrils the spirit of life, and man became a communicating spirit."

Man is a communicating being. If he doesn't have someone to talk to, he talks to himself. Just ask the person who has been in solitary confinement for a while or the castaway who talked to a volleyball named Wilson for four years.

The Power of Communication

Many times we read right over the high value God seems to place on communication. The book of Genesis indicates that God *spoke* things into existence, and later, in Isaiah 1:18 (TLB), God appears to expect dialogue from man when he says, "Come, let's talk this over!" The New Testament refers to Jesus as the *Word* of God. Early philosophical thought dating back before the time of Aristotle recognized that communication was somehow a part of the eternal dimension when it referred to a higher power as *logos*, which means *word*.

Man uses language and communication to accomplish tasks. He names things. Very shortly after man became a communicating spirit, he was given the task to name animals. We understand the power in naming when we realize that we know things by the names we assign them.

Have you ever shopped for a new car? Recently my oldest daughter decided she really liked the robin-egg blue convertible Volkswagen Beetle. One day, just for fun, we pulled into the Volkswagen dealership to look at them. I'm sure you know what I mean when I tell you that after we looked at that new robin-egg blue convertible Volkswagen Beetle, I started seeing robin-egg blue convertible Volkswagen Beetles everywhere! I had no idea so many people owned robin-egg blue convertible Volkswagen Beetles. Now that I have mentioned it so many times, guess how many robin-egg blue convertible Volkswagen Beetles you are going to see over the next few days?

Think for a minute of the names people use to describe you: dad, director, doctor, president, pastor, teacher, athlete, mill worker, electrician, attorney. Though several of the titles might describe you, the one a person chooses to refer to you defines who you are to that person. Names affect both the way you see yourself and the way others see you. In a way, they define you.

But why did God make you a communicating spirit? Just to name things or to accomplish things? If so, why didn't God just make you a manufacturing spirit so you could help Him make things? Or why not a philosophical spirit to help Him think through the intricacies of the universe? Does some drive or power in naming and communicating extend beyond tasks?

Why a communicating spirit? Because God is a communicating Spirit. And by creating us to be communicating spirits, God has created a being in the universe who needs to be known. But if that is true, then God also needs to be known. Exactly!

God Needs to Be Known?

We see a pattern from Genesis all the way to the book of Revelation. It's a pattern of God consistently reaching into the world to touch mankind in a unique way in order to be known. In a broad sense, we a see it in phrases such as "then they will know that I am the LORD," or when the psalmist tells the reader to "make known His [God's] deeds among the peoples."

But we also see this pattern in a very particular and personal way when God makes Himself known to a few men, almost as if He seeks a friend, someone to know Him uniquely. Think of the stories of Abraham, Enoch, Moses, Elijah, and David. God made Himself known to these men in ways He didn't to others.

We see the same thing in the life of Jesus Christ. Jesus made statements to the masses almost as if He was saying, "This is who I am." He said, "I am the bread of life," and "I am the resurrection." And while He continually revealed Himself to groups of people, He had a unique relationship with twelve men, and an even more unique, personal relationship with three of those twelve— Peter, James, and John.

Because God made you and me communicating spirits, we too instinctively reach beyond ourselves. Because we are reflections of God as eternal, creative, communicating spirits, our communication in this world reflects God.

We know that all creation displays God. The earth is full of His beauty, and God saw that each part of His creation was good. He could see Himself. The great current-day theologian N.T. Wright said that creation is always worshipping God and reflecting His character. Creation depicts God's characteristics—His beauty, simplicity, and complexity.

But Dr. Wright argues that mankind is the voice of creation. God made us to worship Him, to verbally speak the wonders and magnificence of the eternal God. And man's unique role is to provide the "because." We are rational beings and endowed with free will, so we evaluate everything we know and perceive about God, and we conclude that "God is great because…!" And we then list all the things we know and have experienced.

Yet man doesn't just express who God is to Him; he also gives voice to the beauty and the wonder of God that the universe displays. God doesn't just look at man and all creation and *see* Himself. He *hears* who He is.

How do we know this? Jesus Himself tells us so. Jesus, the great revealer of God, declared that if we don't worship God, the very rocks will cry out. All nature is made to worship Him, but we were given a very unique task. Out of our own free will and knowledge, we are witnesses in the universe to the wonders of God, and out of our mouths we declare the glory of God—His character. If we won't, inanimate creation will be forced to do so.

Why? Because God is insecure, or because He is an egomaniac? No…not at all. Instead, it is because God needs those He created to freely tell Him who He is.

God needs us to tell Him who He is? In a word, yes. Does that sound odd to you? Read on…

We can say that God needs to be known because the word *need* has two faces. One is to *require,* and the other is to *desire.* God does not need our praise because He requires to be known. God needs our praise because He *desires* to be known. God does not require anything, and certainly not anything from us. But He does have a deep desire for you to know Him. So much so that He has not withheld anything. God loved you so much that He gave everything—including the life of His own Son—so that you could *know* Him and, by knowing Him, know yourself as a spiritual being. An eternal, creative, communicating being.

So if being known is important to God and it is part of His nature, then we can be pretty sure that because we are made in His image we possess the same desire, the same drive.

I have three daughters, and I cannot begin to tell you how much I love them or how important they are to me. From time to time each one makes up her own pet name for me. A few years ago, my middle daughter, Elle, coined a Latin name—Coolius Maximus—and called me by that name when we were having fun and joking around. Lately she started calling me Zeus.

Of course, I am neither Coolius Maximus nor Zeus. Each time Elle comes up with a new name I ask why she chose it, and she rattles off her reasons. As embarrassed as I would be to have others hear her refer to me by those names, I love hearing them from her. Each of my girls helps me see who I am, or perhaps who I can be.

Candidly, I often feel that I fail them as a father. But like most fathers I am so focused on trying to be a *good* father that I just keep going. Occasionally, out of nowhere, one of my daughters will blurt out, "You're a great dad." None of my daughters say it the same way, and they don't all say it at the same time. It appears to be spontaneous. But each time I am taken aback and ask myself, *Really?* even as I'm thinking, *But didn't I just discipline you for something?* Occasionally I will follow up with, "What makes you say that?"

Invariably, she smiles as if to say, "Are you kidding?" She then continues with exaggerated expressions, "Because you do…, you do…, you are…!"

When they tell me that I'm a good dad or that they love me, it touches my heart in a special way because I realize I can do nothing to make them feel that way. If I required an "I love you, Daddy" in order to get dinner, or an essay on why I'm a good father for each movie ticket they receive, their words wouldn't have much meaning. When they choose to talk to me that way, and when they spell out their reasons, I enjoy one of the greatest feelings in my life. I find myself thinking, *Well, if they say that, then maybe I am a good father.* They impact the way I see myself.

Unlike air, food, and water, I do not need their affection and declarations to live. Then do I covet their praise because I am an egomaniac? Because I'm insecure? I may be a little insecure, but that is not why I crave it. I simply desire it. And quite honesty, without it I might be alive, but I will never truly live.

Remember Duke?

In chapter 1 we talked about reaching the end of life only to discover that you missed the target. In chapter 2 I proposed that you are on a quest to be known and that this quest will lead you to both a richer life now, and when you reach death's door, the sense that your life was meaningful. In this chapter I hope you are seeing that the *source* of your quest is God. It was infused into you by the very breath of God. But I couldn't fully disclose one other aspect of this quest until now, and it is this.

You don't begin your quest to discover something. Rather, you start your quest to recover something. Likewise, you don't begin a quest to create. Instead, you embark on a quest to return something to its original condition.

In the legend of King Arthur and his search for the Holy Grail, the knights did not set out to discover the Holy Grail but to recover it. In the Lord of the Rings trilogy, Frodo's quest was not to create a place for the ring to rule all rings. His quest was to return the ring to the fire from which it was formed.

And not just any fire would do, or the molten metal deep within just any mountain. Instead, the ring had to return to a certain mountain. Why?

Because that is where the ring was made. It had to be returned to its point of origin.

What I did not disclose in chapter 2 about your quest is that you are not on a journey to *discover* yourself and to have others discover you as well. You are on a quest to *recover* yourself and to return to the place where you were known.

In the biblical story of creation the first man, Adam, lived in peace in a beautiful garden. Each day, God and Adam would spend some time just hanging out in the garden. Adam didn't seem to have to discover who he was or why he was there. I doubt the question ever crossed his mind. He talked to his Creator on a daily basis and enjoyed his meaningful work of tending the garden and naming the animals.

God didn't just create Adam and say, "Okay, have a good time. Entertain yourself." Man was a purposeful creation with a purpose in creation. If you are a manager, you recognize the fulfillment Adam must have felt when he brought order to his world, something that was a by-product of his creative and communicating spiritual nature. The demands of his body and the desires of his spirit were in equilibrium. But then something changed.

Adam and Eve chose to make their own way. When they made their choice, they knew the penalty but did not suspect the consequence. The penalty was death. The consequence was separation.

Adam and Eve received notice to vacate their home. God evicted them from the place of equilibrium of body and spirit, the place where the needs and appetites of the body were in harmony with the eternal, creative, and communicative nature of the spirit.

Once outside the garden, Adam had to work just to survive. God told Adam he must work the ground from which he was taken, and this work would remind him that he was nothing but dust. His life was a vapor that would arise and pass without meaning. He had become physically separated from his home and meaningful work, and his spirit had become separated from its Creator. In a way he had become separated from himself, which must have produced a sense of estrangement.

Since that time, no man has lived in the garden. Each man is born into the wilderness. Man has become restless because the physical side of life—

working, providing food, and getting ahead—has taken over. We have lost the equilibrium of body and spirit. Our efforts are so focused on surviving that we cannot hear the call of our spirit. Its voice is muted and distant. We have become separated from our sense of being known. We are alone even when we are with others because regardless of how much we talk about sports and the weather, no one knows who we really are. We do a great job of keeping that to ourselves.

Are you on a journey back to the garden? Back to a place where you are known? If so, then like Duke's quest your journey will not be easy, but I believe it will lead you to a sense of peace in your soul. The ironic thing about peace is that it is not won with passivity. The old Latin saying "*Igitur qui desiderat pacem, praeparet bellum*" is translated, "If you want peace, prepare for war." This is the path of your quest.

In the first segment of the *Lord of the Rings* trilogy, we meet a character named Aragorn. Aragorn is of the lineage of a king, but he has become a ranger on Middle-earth, where evil is relentless in its desire to control and defeat the former way of life. Although he has friends and acquaintances, he is a loner. He commands no one, but he has committed himself to protect Frodo. As the story continues, we realize that Middle-earth is separated by factions and old grudges even as evil is uniting under one leader.

In the last segment of the trilogy, Aragorn concludes that Middle-earth does not have enough men to defeat the forces of darkness led by Sauron. In spite of this he is committed to ride to battle. His friend, Elrond, correctly tells him that he rides to battle, but not to victory.

Elrond then encourages Aragorn to set aside previous hurts and grudges and to seek out a certain army of ghosts of the past. This specter army had deserted one of Aragorn's ancestors—a king—in a previous battle, and all the men who deserted were resigned to eternal restlessness. They had to live with their cowardice even in death. Aragorn despised this ghost-army, and he knew that it would never fight for any of Middle-earth's current leaders, and certainly not for him, a mere ranger.

But Elrond again stressed that this army was Middle-earth's only hope. Tired and frustrated, Aragorn reminded his friend that this army would never follow him. "They will follow the king!" Elrond said, revealing the ancient king's sword. The sword had been broken in battle in the first great war, but now gleamed—fully restored—in the light. Elrond then looked Aragorn directly in the eye and said, "Put aside the ranger…become the man you were born to be."

My challenge to you today is to put aside the role you've grown accustomed to and to which you have become resigned. Put it aside. Become the man you were born to be. Rally your previous failures, mistakes, and embarrassments in battle to overcome the forces that want to suppress the power of your spiritual nature and render you a mere (st)ranger roaming the earth alone and unsure of his place.

This is a quest you don't choose; it has already chosen you. You can discount it or ignore it, but you have no other means to quiet the restlessness, isolation, or futility in your life.

And just as Frodo and Aragorn needed others to complete the journey, you too will need certain other people. Even though they are few in number they are absolutely essential, as you will discover in the coming chapters. The path to peace will require that you prepare for war. You will have to do battle for yourself, your family, and your closest friends. It's the stuff movies are made of.

In this chapter we've seen a path God uses to be known. So how do *you* do it? You are a communicating entity and you need to be known, but what is your route? That is what this book is about.

Where do you start? The first place we start is before the beginning, before you entered the world, before the womb. Back when God first knew you. We start with an understanding that your life is not some random event that must somehow find its way. There is already a path.

4

THE PATH

*For the Lord **knows** the way of the righteous,*
but the way of the wicked will perish.
PSALM 1:6

....

IN FEBRUARY 2005, the *Charlotte Observer* sent a reporter to verify rumors of an unusual incident at a local Cracker Barrel restaurant. Susan, a regular breakfast patron, ignited a series of random acts when she quietly paid not only her bill but also that of young man eating alone at table 153. Susan left before the young man realized what had happened.

When the man at table 153 found out what Susan had done, he insisted on paying the bill for Gary and his son, who were seated across from him at table 154. Gary and his son decided to leave ten dollars to cover breakfast for the next person coming in.

When Peggy, the waitress, told the next customer that his bill was paid, he too bought breakfast for the next customer, a woman, who then paid the check for the woman seated at table 131. That person paid the check for the lady at table 141 who said thank you and left.

Peggy watched the events of the morning with a sense of awe. When she heard some people seated at table 123 talking about random acts of kindness, she unknowingly acted as a bridge to a new chain of "picking up the tab." She sat down and told that group about the events of the morning. They listened in amazement and then decided to do the same.

Those people paid the check for the woman at table 133, who subsequently covered the check for the elderly lady at table 114. The woman was so grateful that she paid the bill for a mother and her three children at table 124. That young mother picked up the check for the man in a suit at table 133, who was so appreciative that he told the waitress he wanted to buy breakfast for the woman who had been seated at table 124 after the mother and her children had left. So Peggy plopped herself down in front of that woman—the one newly seated at table 124—and said, "Tag, you're it."

After hearing the whole story, this woman also felt compelled to buy someone's breakfast. As she looked around trying to determine the next lucky recipient, Peggy told her about a young man at table 113. He was very concerned about the price of his meal and had ordered water rather than juice or coffee. He seemed to be counting the pennies in his head as he placed the order. As a result of Peggy's suggestion, the woman at table 124 decided to buy that man's breakfast.

When he had finished his breakfast the young man asked for his check. That's when Peggy told him not to worry about it, saying, "The woman who just left paid your bill." She said nothing about the events of the morning.

According to the newspaper, the young man said, "Gosh, thanks! That was nice of her." Then he left. The chain of random acts that Susan had started lasted six hours, and Peggy conceded to the reporter that the day had been truly amazing. Then she said, "I figured this whole thing happened so that young man could have breakfast."

As I read this story I felt good about the random acts of kindness. One person's good works can prompt others to do the same, and that is a great lesson for each of us.

But what was even more interesting was that Peggy viewed the events of the morning not as random acts of kindness as much as a way to pay for that last young man's breakfast. Maybe some things aren't so random after all. Though an act may seem random to the actor, could it be connected to some overall purpose?

The Kernel of Intention

This story may seem unrelated to your quest to be known, but intention is actually at the heart of your quest. I hope the previous chapters helped you recognize that you will be restless until you engage your quest to be known, and I hope you are now readying yourself for that journey. Future chapters will lay out the journey of being known, but first we must establish that this is not some random, scattered game of hide-and-seek. This is not a scavenger hunt for meaningless trinkets. You have been called to this quest by name.

Why do I think so? Consider the big picture—the universe—and work down from there. If the universe is random, perhaps we are too. But if we discern some sort of intention in the formation of the universe, we must at least consider that God also created each of us intentionally.

The Intentional Universe

For centuries scientists assumed the universe was eternal. They believed it had always existed. But midway into the twentieth century, mounting evidence required scientists to theorize some sort of beginning or starting point for the universe. Their conclusion was that somehow—about 14 billion years ago—a random combination of chemicals converged and ignited, triggering what would become our universe.

Science also believed a similar random and spontaneous process produced the simplest form of life on earth, which ultimately led to you. Therefore, you are random. And you are pretty much at the mercy of genetic combinations produced by a random marriage, the environment in which you happened to grow up, and the arbitrary options and choices that come your way.

Or are you?

The past decade or so witnessed a subtle shift in scientific thought. As researchers developed increasingly sophisticated models to analyze the conditions necessary for random development of the universe, many started to realize that the math didn't add up. Even 14 billion years did not provide enough time to produce what we see today if everything was left to chance.

Around the same time, scientists who study the universe began to ask, how did the universe find the miniscule path between collapsing in on itself and expanding indefinitely? While accepting the possibility that a random fluctuation set the universe in motion, many scientists realized the margin for error in the rate at which the universe expanded is so razor thin that the chance of it happening as the result of a random chemical reaction is highly suspicious. In his book the *Nature of Time and Space*, renowned physicist Stephen Hawking stated this:

> If the rate of expansion one second after the [hot] big bang had been less by one part in ten billion, the universe would have collapsed after a few million years. If it had been greater by one part in ten billion, the universe would have been essentially empty after a few million years.

Consequently, random theory migrated toward complexity theory, which claims that simple organisms and systems *try* to organize into more complex organisms and systems.

Complexity theory runs somewhat counter to the second law of thermodynamics. That principle essentially states that matter in a closed system eventually tends toward decay rather than development. Think of corrosion and rust. Underground pipes don't get newer over time, they deteriorate. You don't get younger. Your body ages until it eventually wears out. So if it runs counter to a law of physics, what is the appeal of complexity theory?

I am terrible at golf, but my wife is pretty good. She doesn't get a chance to play very often, but she really enjoys the game. We played a couple of times during our first year of marriage, and one day she hit a hole in one on the fourth hole. I was amazed, and she was understandably thrilled.

Now, imagine that she tees off on the fifth hole and the same thing happens. She hits another hole in one. That would really be amazing, wouldn't it? But if she did it again on the sixth and then on the seventh, I don't think I would be as amazed as I would be suspicious.

Many scientists moved from amazement to suspicion with the random model of life. Complexity theory provided a compelling alternative to scientists because it recognized the odds against random chemical combinations producing the exact match required to form the complex chemical chains of life. Not the odds against those random combinations happening once, but the odds against them happening over and over again in precise succesion.

Still, even though complexity theory math models begin to offer a more plausible explanation, they end like those of random theory because although the model incorporates the idea that organisms seek to organize, the universe has not existed long enough for complexity theory to work. According to Gerald Schroeder, who holds a doctoral degree from MIT, the odds of it happening are even less than the odds that you will win the state lottery this week...and the next...then the next...and again the next. At some point lottery officials will get suspicious of your "luck," just as I would if my wife had six consecutive holes in one.

Perhaps that is why 80-year-old philosophy professor Antony Flew, previously an ardent defender of atheism, recently reversed his position. After he spent a lifetime touting the legitimacy of atheism, Dr. Flew concluded that the scientific community's current understanding of the complexity of life makes his previous position indefensible. The universe must have had a first cause. Someone had to intentionally start it.

More and more scientists today believe that the only explanation for both life and the universe is, for lack of a better term, intentional complexity. In other words, simple organisms not only tend to develop into more complex organisms, but some sort of code directs that development. Some sort of clue—an inherent direction—allows organisms to be more inclined to one combination than others. When intention is factored into a model of the development of the universe and the life within it, the math works.

You might think, *Sure, there is a direction to the universe and to life in general. But God doesn't have a unique direction for my life and at the same time every other person's life. That's far too complex.*

Yes, it is complex. But science and Scripture agree on the unique nature of each life. That fact is undisputed.

Leaving a Trail or Following a Path

When I was young, some of my favorite television shows were *Dragnet, Adam 12,* and *The FBI.* In many of the episodes a suspect was linked to a crime scene by his fingerprints, providing proof that he was there. This was possible, of course, because everyone's fingerprints are different.

Today, shows like *CSI* and *Cold Case* dramatize the use of DNA to connect perpetrators to their victims, often after many years have passed. We even see retinal scans routinely used to provide access to secure and restricted areas. Clearly, a person's unique fingerprints, DNA, and retina leave a distinctive trail as he passes through time. And even though we leave a trail as we live our lives, I sense that God also lays out a path before us. A particular path for each of us to follow.

If each one of us alive today is unique, the logical conclusion is that each life also possesses a unique direction. If God intended to place specific qualities and traits in your life, surely He realized that He would predispose you to a certain course.

In the Scriptures, God spoke to the prophet Jeremiah and said, "Before I formed you in the womb I knew you, and before you were born I consecrated you." Before this man was born, even before the womb, God had a plan for his life. He set him aside before he had any form or substance and said, "This is Jeremiah. He will be born at this specific time, and he will be My prophet."

Was Jeremiah an exception? Jesus said that God is aware of a single sparrow falling from the sky. He was making a point that God is mindful of each life. No one is insignificant. Jesus then spoke directly to His disciples and said, "Even the hairs of your head are numbered." Later, the apostle Paul told a group of Greek philosophers at the Areopagus that God appoints men to live at certain times and specific places.

If God is aware of you—if God knows you—then you can be certain that He must also have an underlying intention for your life. And His intention for your life precedes your own efforts. You don't have to create meaning from nothing. God already did that. He created the universe from nothing, and He created you from nothing. He formed the universe intentionally, providing it with intrinsic direction, and He formed you intentionally, infusing your life with direction. You will either align yourself with that direction and find harmony or resist it and face dissonance. Satisfaction will elude you.

I suspect that something in you already knows that God has a purpose for your life. In the wee hours of the morning as you lie in bed half awake and half asleep, do you ever hear the faint *beep...beep...beep* of a homing beacon? It may be dim. You might not hear it very often. But I believe you have become aware of its distinct sound. Like the signal from a black box on a downed airplane, the beacon you hear is attached to a black box of intention buried in the depths of your being.

In most cases God's intention for your life is not simply about a specific job or career. It is not the same thing as fatalism or determinism, which gives you no real freedom to do what you wish. It is about a certain path. A path that you—His creation—feel most natural following. Why? Because it corresponds to a deep-seated sense of direction, as if at some point in the distant past someone quietly whispered the directions in your ear and also mentioned landmarks you would see along the way.

> O LORD, you have searched me and known me!
> You know when I sit down and when I rise up;
> you discern my thoughts from afar.
> You search out my path and my lying down
> and are acquainted with all my ways.
> Even before a word is on my tongue,
> behold, O LORD, you know it altogether.
> You hem me in, behind and before,
> and lay your hand upon me…
> My frame was not hidden from you,
> when I was being made in secret,
> intricately woven in the depths of the earth.
> Your eyes saw my unformed substance;
> in your book were written, every one of them,
> the days that were formed for me,
> when as yet there were none of them (Psalm 139:1-5,15-16).

The city of Eugene, Oregon, is laced with jogging trails. Jogging is as much a part of the culture of Eugene as country music is part of Nashville.

When I was in Eugene one spring day, I watched an older gentleman walk his dog along one of the paths. Few other people were on the same path that day, and the dog sniffed bushes and tree trunks on the one side of the path and then chased a chipmunk on the other.

The dog's leash was retractable, but it could be as long as 20 feet when fully extended. This gave the dog a lot of freedom, while allowing the man to maneuver around obstacles. Occasionally a jogger would approach from the opposite direction, and the older man would slowly and gently recoil the leash, subtly drawing the dog toward him. In short order the dog was safely trotting alongside the man. When the jogger had passed safely by, the dog resumed his exploration. All the while, the two moved down the path and toward home.

The Advantage of Intention

It occurred to me that—at least theoretically—the dog really didn't have to follow the path. Neither was it required to follow the old man home. Though the dog only weighed about 25 pounds, it could have struggled and tugged on the leash until the man let go. Or perhaps it could have chewed on the leash and eventually broken free. One way or the other, the dog could have left to make its own way. It could choose to go wherever it wanted, not being confined to the things that occurred along the path.

But there is something sad about a dog running loose on its own. Once in a while you see one scared half out of its wits as it tries to cross a four-lane freeway, dodging speeding cars and wondering what went wrong.

A few years ago I heard a noise outside our house in the middle of the night. I suspected it came from raccoons I had seen from time to time, so I went outside to chase them away. Instead, I discovered a mongrel dog eating garbage out of my tipped-over trash can. It jumped and ran away as I opened the door. Driving away the next morning, I saw trash scattered around several of the neighbors' side doors, a clear indication that they had been unwitting benefactors of the hungry dog.

After a few nights of the same drill, someone called animal control. Within a couple of days, workers picked up the dog and took it to the animal shelter, where the dog was probably eventually put to sleep. No one knew the dog. No one came to claim it. Clearly, the dog didn't realize how different its life would have been if someone had known it—especially at the end. But I suspect that somehow Duke—the dog we met in chapter 2—knew the difference.

Black and White

I think most of us want to be on a path. We want to sense that we are being led because if we are, at the end of the day, we are more likely to arrive home. Psychologists tell us that people are most comfortable when they have boundaries. Having a sense of direction is a sign of good mental health.

But does a path preclude freedom to chose? Is my freedom limited to choosing or rejecting God's intention for my life? Or, if I truly believe that my choices seriously impact my life, do I have to give up the ideal of an intrinsic direction...a destiny?

Logically, they are in conflict. They are black and white. How can you choose and at the same time have the choice made for you? Can you be free to decide even as you are being directed? The short answer is yes—I truly believe so.

Scientists have discovered that light has a very unusual property. Depending on how it is measured, light can be both a wave and a particle. When a technician investigates the nature of light with the preconception that it is a wave, that is what he finds. Light is a wave. If a researcher tests for particles, light will appear to have the properties of a particle. The peculiar characteristic of light to be both a wave and a particle is a little baffling to many of us. Light is clearly unique.

Just as light is at once both a wave and a particle, your life is filled with both freedom and intention. Your life is an adventure on an uncharted course, bursting with choices and shaped by significant relationships. Yet at the same time, God created you intentionally, and you are following an internal compass.

The dog I saw in Eugene, Oregon, seemed to give little thought to the directional influence of the older man with the leash. The dog made many choices as he moved back and forth across the path. He marked his trail. He smelled the plants. He snacked on the occasional litter and chased chipmunks. All the while, the dog was moving forward along the path.

Intentionality

Why do I use the word *intentionality*? Why don't I just use the word *purpose* instead? Aren't intention and purpose the same thing?

Intention and purpose are indeed very similar. In my opinion, intention is more closely associated with the beginning of an action or process, whereas purpose refers to the destination or end result. The United States judicial system sometimes refers to a certain class of crimes as intentional crimes. A jury cannot find you guilty of an intentional crime if the prosecutor cannot establish intent. For example, you cannot be convicted of first-degree murder unless the district attorney first proves you intended to commit the act that resulted in murder.

You see intentionality every Monday night on television. If you watch the NFL Monday night football game you know that coaches or quarterbacks call each play with the intention of moving the ball toward the goal. The eleven players on the team have specific duties and tasks, and each one interacts differently with both defensive and offensive players. Each player has unique intentionality while the team works toward a common purpose. Scripture says a similar thing this way:

> And we know that for those who love God all things work together for good, for those who are called according to his purpose. For those whom he foreknew he also predestined [intention, desire] to be conformed to the image of his Son [intentionality, the process], in order that he might be the firstborn among many brothers [purpose, result] (Romans 8:28-29).

What Is My Path?

God was intentional when He made you, and His intention is inseparable from who you are. You are tethered to a path. The question naturally follows, what is that path?

I cannot tell you what your specific path is because I don't know who you are. Other people do know you, and I hope you are beginning to realize that these people will play a crucial role in shaping the direction of your life. But they don't chart your course. They don't determine your path.

Though I can't tell you what your unique path is, I can tell you what it is about. The eleven players on a football team have unique routes, but they have a single purpose. They are assigned routes based on a common intention. The wide receiver does not run his route while carrying a baseball mitt just in case a baseball game breaks out. No one on the field has a chessboard in his pocket. The ball, the field, and the rules determine the actions of each player, and their actions will always correspond to the ball, the field, and the rules.

Likewise, your path in life will correspond to tasks, relationships, and character development. By this I mean that God intends for you to do certain things, to influence certain people, and to be transformed into the image of his Son.

This chapter and chapter 9 are about your assignment. God has appointed you to go and bear fruit in this life (John 15:16). Your fruit is directly related to your character, but it may also be the result of a specific task done at a specific time. Or you may produce fruit through a series of tasks over a period of years.

The Trampled Path

Some men can spend a great deal of time trying to figure out what they want to do with their lives. They sense a pressure to know where they are going even at an early age. Other guys never struggle with it. They just seem to be in the right place at the right time, and things happen for them with little apparent effort.

When I was in high school, a classmate had already decided he wanted to be an airline pilot. Everything he did and every class he took somehow seemed to correspond with the desire to be a pilot. I wasn't that way.

My father worked in a lumber mill six days a week and was the pastor of a local church on Sunday. At times I felt I was destined to be a mill worker, and other times I thought I was supposed to be a preacher. I seemed to have a natural ability in business, but I didn't pay much attention to it. I did a lot of different jobs between the ages of 14 and 40. Some—like live television production—I enjoyed more than others, like weeding potato fields.

By my late thirties I sensed I had become a generalist. I was the kind of guy who could do many different things, though I often felt I didn't do anything particularly well. About that time I was on staff at a local church. One day, in an informal staff meeting, the senior pastor made an off-the-cuff and metaphorical statement that I was the best athlete on the team. I think most of us knew what he meant by the statement: I could play any position, but perhaps I was not the best at any position.

Several years later I was writing a brief personal bio for a work project, and I started to laugh. In the paragraphs profiling my life, I clearly saw the three stands of ministry, communication, and business woven through my life. I only *looked* like a generalist because my path was pretty wide, and it took a little time to trample down the grass, so to speak. But the path was unmistakable.

I spent a few moments reflecting and realized that the projects and tasks I most remembered from my youth—the occasional areas of academic success and the jobs I most enjoyed—were each obvious data points. Each one helped me plot the direction of my life. Individually they were unremarkable, but together they formed a three-stranded cord woven through the years of my life.

Can you see a pattern in your life? Look back at the path leading from your childhood to today. Which memories are strongest? Where were you the most successful? What kind of person were you drawn to? Do your memories, successes, relationships, dreams, and even failures reveal a path?

Several years ago I did a research project for a church. The pastor was trying to discern how to develop the church website, so I used a small number of one-on-one interviews, a number of in-depth questionnaires, and a more broadly distributed short-form questionnaire to find out how church staff, members, and attendees used the Internet. But in addition to how they used the Web, I wanted to know who these people were, how involved they were at church, their dominant style of communication, and the role faith played in their life. The people who filled out either one of the questionnaires could mail them after they were completed, or they could drop them into designated baskets at the church.

I was scheduled to deliver a paper summarizing the results of this project to an academic conference before giving it to the pastor, so I input the data into the statistical software program as it came in rather than waiting for all of the questionnaires to be returned. The day before I was to stand up and deliver the results in a speech, about 90 percent of the questionnaires had been returned. But the months of planning and work had merely determined that church members indeed used the Internet, which was not exactly a groundbreaking concept.

The next day I stood up at the conference and delivered a 20-minute speech that essentially said church members used the Internet. The analysis of the data seemed to indicate that none of the really interesting theories or member characteristics mattered. None of the factors that drove the research for the church or that enticed colleagues to attend the lecture seemed to have any effect. People involved in the research and those attending the lecture were disappointed because they really hoped to find patterns in Internet use and motivations for use. I still expected to find a pattern.

Over the following two weeks the remaining questionnaires came in. Through previous research I learned that sometimes a pattern isn't recognized simply because not enough data had been collected to make the connection significant. So, though it seemed meaningless and futile to others, I entered the remaining data. When all the questionnaires were in and after entering all the data, I ran the same statistical tests I had run before. The results were completely different.

The data from last few questionnaires had made the difference between no pattern—no connection between Internet use, personal data, communication traits, and religiosity—and a clear pattern. The connections I expected to find were there after all, and as a result, the study had gone from meaningless to meaningful. Had we failed to look at all the data we would have reached the wrong conclusion, so I was glad to be able to submit the correct conclusion to the church when the time came. I also resubmitted the research paper.

Your life pattern may not yet be clear. Even though you *hope* your life has a direction, you may not yet *see* the path of intention. But the path is there. You just may not have enough data to identify it.

Don't reach the wrong conclusion. And don't just hope a path will emerge. To live life with confidence, you can't just hope the path exists. You must know the path is there, and you must look for it. A professor of sociology named Ivan Illich once said, "We must rediscover the distinction between hope and expectation." As you reflect on your hopes and your expectations in life, you may rediscover your path. It is there.

An Unrecognized Path

I met Thomas in Southern California in the early 1980s when we were both youth ministers. Thomas also sold automobiles during the week, and in the course of selling vehicles he invariably met people going through tough times. Thomas commonly prayed with two or three complete strangers every week.

Thomas is a very likable man, and he was very successful selling cars, so when he and his young wife had a child, Thomas was earning enough money to buy a nice home. Little by little, Thomas found the demands of work squeezing out his duties as a youth pastor, and within a couple years he gave up his job at the church.

I lost touch with Thomas in California in the late 1980s and didn't see him until a couple weeks before Christmas 2002, when we bumped into each other at a school function in Franklin, Tennessee. In that brief conversation I discovered that Thomas had become an auto broker, and he had continued to earn a good living for his family.

For the past three years, Thomas and I have had breakfast or lunch every few months. We came to realize that he was conflicted with his role of selling cars because he still desired to be involved in some sort of ministry. I sensed he felt that he had missed God's path for him. He viewed his job with contempt and said he needed to find a way to begin doing what God really wanted him to do—ministry. So even though he had purchased property for his own car lot, he leased the property out to other people. To establish his own lot would tether Thomas to the car business.

When we last had lunch, I saw a major change in Thomas. He quickly confessed that he had been doing a lot of soul-searching, and he realized that he had bought into the idea that being a car salesman was somehow beneath him. But as he leaned across the table in the crowded restaurant, Thomas looked right into my eyes and said, "I looked back over my life and realized being a car salesman allowed me to do the very thing I love to do."

He continued, "I meet people who need someone they can trust to help them buy a car. If I can do that, then great. If not, at least I can pray with them and encourage them. That's what I love!"

Being a car salesman was not keeping Thomas from his ministry—from his path. Instead, it was part of his path.

The Restraint of the Path

A person could argue that all I'm describing is a pattern that develops as the result of choices, not a path of intention. That is certainly an explanation. But if a man's path is simply the sum of his choices, and if there is no outside intent attached to those choices, then he should be able to walk away from his path without experiencing any consequence or intervention.

Tim and I were childhood friends. One Friday night when we were young, he spent the night at my house. After playing games until late in the night, we stretched out on the two twin beds in my darkened room and quietly talked.

Tim's father, Lonnie, owned a small heating and air conditioning company, and he was very active in the community and in our local church. Tim told me that several years before, when Tim's older brother and sister were very small, business was tough, and his dad had thought that maybe he should do something else with his life. Perhaps he should get a fresh start somewhere else. Tim told me that, during that time, Lonnie considered moving his family to a small town on the northern California coast so he could go into business with his brother Bug, a deep-sea fisherman. Lonnie and Bug decided they would work together for three weeks, and if it went well, Lonnie and his family would move there.

The time came for Lonnie to give it a try, so he left his wife and two young children at home in Klamath Falls and drove to the coast to start fishing with his brother. That first Sunday morning together they set out to sea very early and had every reason to believe the fishing would be great. As they moved down the coast a bit, Bug asked Lonnie to keep his hand on the till of the ship while he went below to check on the newly installed engine.

At six in the morning, as the ship moved toward another fishing area, Lonnie heard an audible voice say, "Go home—your family needs you." The voice was so clear he thought maybe Bug had yelled up at him from the engine room, but as he peered into the hull he realized his brother was fast at work and had not said a word.

When Bug came back up on deck Lonnie was tempted to ask him if he heard the voice, but Lonnie was sure his brother would think he was crazy. So they continued to fish.

The ships all around them were hauling in salmon, but Lonnie and his brother caught just a couple of fish. By noon, Bug commented that he was baffled. As he moved to the front of the ship, Lonnie once again heard a voice—as if coming from a man standing next to him—that said, "Go home! Your family needs you."

That same Sunday afternoon a man stopped by Lonnie's house in Klamath Falls and asked Lonnie's wife, Ann, for some money. Ann's initial response was to say no. But she reconsidered as she recalled the Scripture urging people to be hospitable because, in doing so, sometimes they entertained angels without even knowing it. So Ann tried to get the man some help at her church and a local gospel mission, but it didn't work out.

Meanwhile, Lonnie and Bug were wrapping up their day of fishing. Lonnie took a small boat ashore with the meager catch, while Bug secured the larger boat and prepped it for the next day. Finally, the two men cleaned what they had, took it to the local market for sale, and headed home.

Back in Klamath Falls, at about 6:00 that evening, Lonnie's wife decided to give the transient man a hot meal on the back porch and then asked him to move on. As the man ate his meal on the porch, Ann heard him ask her young children where their daddy was. They innocently said, "Oh, he's over at the coast. He won't be back for three weeks."

On the California coast 250 miles away, Lonnie and Bug sat down with Bug's wife to eat dinner. It was 6:00 in the evening. As they prepared to serve the food, Lonnie heard the voice once again, but this time it just said, "Go home now!"

Immediately Lonnie stood up, grabbed his bags, and headed for the door. Bug was startled and said, "Where are you going?"

Lonnie replied, "I'm going home."

"But we agreed that you'd give this three weeks before you decided," Bug said, with an astonished look on his face.

"I have to go home now," was all Lonnie could say, as he slammed the door behind him.

The weather was bad, and Lonnie didn't get home until nearly midnight. He was surprised to see the kitchen light on, and as he walked in, Ann said, "I am *so* glad you're home!"

Ann then proceeded to tell Lonnie the events of the day and added, "I think he's coming back here tonight." Lonnie assured her that the man would not return. They turned off the kitchen light and went to bed.

The lights in the house had been out for just a short time when Lonnie and Ann heard the doorknob turning on the back door. The moon was full and shone brightly on the house, so as Lonnie rose from his bed and entered the hallway he could see the silhouette of the man at the back door. Lonnie grabbed a shotgun from the gun closet in the hallway and reached the back door just as the man was opening it.

The startled man said, "I didn't expect to see you here."

"I bet you didn't," Lonnie chuckled, as he pulled the hammers of the shotgun back, causing them to make a loud *click-click* in the stillness of the night.

They exchanged a few brief words, and Lonnie raised the gun toward the stranger and in his gravelly voice said, "Brother, you better turn around and go right back where you came from, or I'll blow a hole in you so big you'll crawl right back through it!"

Meanwhile, Ann had called the police and a patrol car happened to be about a mile away, so the man was picked up by the police just two minutes later. The next day Lonnie sat down and wrote Bug a letter explaining that he would not be moving to the coast. Instead, Lonnie enrolled in Bible school.

Three weeks later Lonnie received a letter from his brother's wife. In the letter, Lonnie read that when Bug discovered Lonnie wasn't coming back, he made a deal with a new partner, and they quickly left to fish. Bug never returned. The letter said that Bug's ship, together with seven others, was caught in a hurricane off the coast of Baja, California, and sank.

I don't know Lonnie's path, but I do know that he believed he had one and that God kept him on it. Lonnie influenced my life and many others in Klamath Falls for many years.

A Critical Clarification

Before we finish this chapter and move on, I must make one clarification: There are actually two life paths. These two paths are distinct and diametrically opposed, and they correspond to two different groups of people. The two groups are the righteous and the wicked, and the two paths are intentionality and instrumentality. You can not be in both groups any more than a woman can be both pregnant and not pregnant. Either intentionality is in you or it is not.

Let's start by considering the second group—the wicked. Few people think of themselves as wicked even though they may admit to doing things that fit the description. Perhaps we can use words like *aimless* or *purposeless*. People may gain the whole world and be international celebrities. But in the end they return to dust, and within three or four generations their accomplishments are like chaff in the wind. They don't belong to a higher purpose, and they die unknown (in the eternal sense).

The path of the wicked is instrumentality. By that I mean they are mere tools—instruments for someone else's use. Scripture says that God uses a king or a nation as an instrument of discipline for the righteous. The wicked are nameless, faceless individuals God leaves to their own folly and to the futility of their own thinking, except when they can be used to reward or discipline one of His children. Otherwise, Scripture says, God laughs at their plans, for they have no control over the future. Their path leads nowhere.

The other group is the righteous, and the path of the righteous man is one of intention. In this book, I make a very big assumption. I assume you are either one of the righteous or you are seeking that path. How can I make that assumption?

Because deep calls to deep. This is not a simple book. The idea that you are on a quest to be known makes no sense to a person who ultimately sees only himself. The man who recognizes no higher purpose values control. To him, intentionality violates the impression of personal power and subordinates man, creating the perception of weakness. Living the life of an animal and elevating strength and will is simpler than engaging the questions of the heart. But if you have read this far, you are not looking for simple answers. You want to go deeper.

Beware

As you climb the mountain of being known you must realize that though many paths lead up that mountain, only one leads to the summit. It is your path. Along the way you will recognize the faces of many people, some who are in your life now and others who were in your past. Some will be comforting. Others will not. A few people will remain in the shadows. They are specific individuals you expect to meet up with in the future. As we'll see in future chapters, in each of these cases you may find yourself confronted with a choice.

Frequently, blizzards on this mountain can create whiteout conditions. For that reason a few select people are placed along your path to serve as guides or resources. Without them you will either get lost on the mountain or run out of supplies. This book will enable you to more consistently recognize them when you see them.

But you will face something far more sinister than blizzards. If you truly are on a quest to be known, then you have to know about a force that is bent on preventing you from succeeding. Because you need to be known, the focus of the attack is to make you question who you are. You are being set up.

5

THE DETOUR

*Then Jacob gave Esau bread and lentil stew,
and he ate and drank and rose and went **his** way.
Thus Esau despised his birthright.*

GENESIS 25:34

....

SEVERAL DECADES AGO my brother-in-law told me about a group of guys he knew that decided they wanted to go bow hunting for Kodiak bear in Alaska. The idea of hunting such a powerful animal with a bow and arrow was tantalizing, and the more they talked about it the more excited they became. Their intensity grew until they could almost feel the icy wind in their faces and see the magnificent beast poised on a mountain crag above them. The five hunters decided they would do it the coming season.

When the group applied for their bow hunting permits, they were told all the available permits had been issued, but they could get permits for hunting bear with a gun. The men were disappointed because they felt rifles would take the challenge out of the hunt, yet the call of the wild prevailed, so they set out for Alaska.

The group traveled the back roads over rough terrain in an old truck on their way to where they would set out on foot. As they rounded a curve on a narrow road, one man glanced down the steep ravine and saw a big male Kodiak bear about 150 yards downhill—just across a mountain stream. He yelled out, and the truck skidded to a stop.

In a flash the men grabbed their rifles and jumped out of the truck. The smallest rifle in the group was a 30.06. The man who spotted the bear raised his rifle, lined up the big bear in the crosshairs of his scope, and pulled the trigger.

The bear jerked his massive head and shoulders upward as the bullet reached its mark. The next shot hit just a second later, and the bear roared in anger as he twisted his head the opposite direction, trying to locate the source of the attack. By the time the fourth bullet was released he had spotted the five men on the ridge high above him, and before the fifth bullet had left its chamber the bear was crossing the stream toward the steep hill.

The bear moved up the hill toward the hunters at an incredible speed, and each man began firing his rifle as quickly as he could. The bear continued upward as if the bullets were made of rubber, rapidly closing the gap between the bear and the hunters. The only man left with any bullets in his rifle squeezed off his last round as the four other men worked feverishly to reload. The giant bear finally dropped about 20 feet from the group. The hunters had used every bullet in all five guns to bring down a wounded bear running up steep terrain. My brother-in-law said the men never again talked about using a bow and arrow to hunt Kodiak bear.

The men returned from the hunt much more sober men than when they left for the adventure. One man's hair turned completely white within three months of his hunt. The men challenged a formidable foe, but it wasn't a sport for the bear. When a hunter decides to breach the lair of a beast, he must be conscious of the potential to fall prey to the thing he hunts, to turn in an instant from hunter to hunted.

Likewise, if you are on a quest to be known, you must realize that the path is not without risk. You will face dangers from without and within. You have an adversary who seeks to destroy you using a time-tested and proven battle plan. He will try to detour you by distracting you with your appetites or by discouraging you with failure and disappointment. If neither of these methods takes you out of the game, he will ambush you at the point of your purpose.

A Strategy of Deception

My wife and I recently watched Charles Stanley on his *In Touch* television program. Dr. Stanley said that God has set each of us on a path, but we are often led off course by a simple but clever trick. He picked up a compass and said that the compass is designed to help you find your way by using a small metal needle to point north. A compass is built to detect the pull of the magnetic north pole.

But Dr. Stanley pointed out that if he were to place a small magnetic rod beside the compass, the rod would pull the needle toward it, effectively pointing the user in the wrong direction. This would seem like an obvious move by our enemy, but many times we miss it because we get so busy with the day-to-day duties of life that more and more time passes between each glimpse of the compass. Perhaps our best defense is to know what Satan uses to pull us off the path. Specifically, what is the magnetic rod in your life?

If Satan is anything, he is consistent. He uses the same strategy over and over because it works so well most of the time. For instance, in this chapter we will see that Satan's tactic is to detour you by baiting you with your appetites. So, if we know his tactic and the bait he intends to use, what is his objective?

Satan's objective is to steal and then destroy your identity. If he can do so, you are as good as dead. Remember the riddle, "If a tree falls in the forest and nobody hears it, does it make a sound?" You may be physically alive, yet if the true person God made you to be can remain in the shadows—unknown by you, by those around you, and by God—does the fact that you ever lived really matter?

Satan's strategy is simple, and it is effective because we never see it coming. We take the bait every time. The bait distracts us enough to detour us from our path, and before we know it we have traded away our identity in an attempt to satisfy what we discover is an insatiable appetite.

In a June 2005 front-page story in *USA Today*, former heavyweight boxing champion Mike Tyson admitted, "The weed got me." As the youngest heavyweight champion in history at age 20, "Iron Mike" seemed unbeatable. Though Tyson's life and career are in ruins and he has been transformed from an icon to a caricature, most people still believe he was unbeatable by any opponent...that is, any opponent other than himself.

In the interview with *USA Today*, Tyson discussed the three things that seem to define his life: drugs, lack of self-esteem, and sexual addiction. In other words, the battle between his appetites and his identity.

Distracted by Appetites

An appetite is a good thing. It reminds us that we are hungry and need food, which is important because we don't eat just once in our lifetime or once a year. We don't even eat once a week or once a day. Our appetite for food is never really satisfied because we must receive nourishment each day, and our appetite ensures we will remember to seek food. But sometimes our appetite becomes hyperactive and compulsive. What was designed as an impulse becomes overpowered and out of control.

I remember watching one of the early episodes of the ABC sitcom *Home Improvement* featuring Tim Allen. The character Tim played in the situation comedy believed the answer to everything was more power. In this particular episode, Tim decided to improve the efficiency of the dishwasher by switching its factory-installed motor with a high-performance motor that could power a riding lawn mower. While a high-performance engine might work great in a lawn mower, it isn't made for a dishwasher. It produces far too much power. Consequently, the first time Tim's wife used the "improved" dishwasher, the overpowered motor burned it out, and the dishwasher became useless.

A similar thing will happen in your life if your appetite becomes too high-powered or attached to something it wasn't intended to run. It will burn you out and cause you to be ineffective. It will divert time, energy, and resources away from your quest.

An Overpowered Appetite

In the mid 1980s, I was very busy in my little world of business. I worked 60 hours a week for a company in Pasadena, California, but my entrepreneurial spirit drove me to start a business services company with two highly talented friends in the nearby town of Arcadia. My primary job gave me Thursdays off, so each week on Thursday I caught a predawn flight out of Orange County, serviced accounts for my company in the Bay Area, and caught a 5:30 PM flight back to Orange County just in time to attend one of my three weekly courses at a law school in Fullerton. Each day started early and ended very late.

I had always been a big coffee drinker, but I soon found myself drinking 50 to 60 cups a day. I didn't always have an opportunity to eat, but I could drink coffee while I worked, drove, or sat in class. After buying out my partners, I sold my company to a small publicly traded company, and I was offered an executive position with them. The new position allowed me to spend more time in the office, and consequently I had more time for lunch. But by Christmas that year, I realized I hadn't cut back on coffee at all.

Drinking coffee is fine. And drinking a lot of coffee during a particularly busy period of time might be understandable. But you don't have to be a nutritional expert to know that drinking 50 cups a day for years on end is not a good thing. And not only that—my identity had become tethered to coffee.

For my birthday and at Christmas, friends and family typically gave me coffee, coffee mugs, coffee gift cards, coffee club memberships, coffee makers, or personalized coffee thermoses. I realized that coffee was no longer a beverage but an appetite that was out of control, and it had been fused with my identity. It drove my day from start to finish.

On New Year's Day, 1987, I stopped drinking coffee completely for 60 days to prove to myself and to others that I could. What a headache I had! For the first three weeks I had no energy at all, and I often had difficulty focusing. I also discovered I was so accustomed to holding a cup in my hands that I felt lost without one, so I started drinking hot water in order to have a surrogate in my hands.

After about a month I found myself eating better because the coffee didn't squelch my appetite. I enjoyed food more. I started using vitamins and felt more like exercising. I realized that I actually felt better.

Isn't it amazing that something can become such a part of you for so long that you cannot separate it from who you are? Often you can't recognize all the ways it controlled you until it is gone. Appetites are powerful because they are designed to keep us alive. But out of context and out of control they do just the opposite. They kill us. Perhaps that is why Jesus was driven to fast at the very beginning of His ministry. His appetites needed to be under control.

Is It Really About Food?

Scripture tells us that when Jesus was baptized, a voice from heaven said, "This is my beloved Son, with whom I am well-pleased." One could say that Jesus heard from God and was compelled to begin His ministry. But instead of forming a 501(c)(3) nonprofit corporation and printing letterhead and business cards with His name and title—Jesus of Nazareth, Son of God— Jesus was led by the Spirit into a wilderness time during which He fasted for 40 days.

At the end of the fast, Satan confronted Jesus with a reasonable request— he asked Jesus to eat something. Where is the diabolical scheme here? Why would Satan waste his time telling Jesus to eat... and who could fault Jesus for eating? Jesus had chosen to not eat, and so He could also choose to eat at any point. There was no sin in eating. But Satan is subtle, and often we have to look behind what he does to discover what he is doing.

When our enemy attacks us in a time of particular vulnerability—such as hunger or pain—he does so by questioning who we are. Jesus was at the threshold of His public ministry. He had no corporate sponsors, and other than John the Baptist, it seems that no one recognized Him or offered letters of introduction. Perhaps even Satan was uncertain that Jesus was the Messiah because so many men emerged over the previous decades claiming the title. Was this Satan's chance to know for sure?

"If you are the Son of God," said Satan, "command these stones to become loaves of bread."

Oh! This isn't really about eating, is it? Hunger was not the real issue. Jesus was particularly vulnerable because His appetite was at a fever pitch. If Jesus would later use a few loaves and fishes to feed 5000 men, why couldn't He use a few stones to feed Himself?

Because Satan's attack—*did Jesus know who He was?*—was hidden in a seemingly benign request—*satisfy Your appetite.* The food was the means to prove His identity to Himself and to others. If Jesus had the slightest doubt about who He was, this was the chance to know for sure. If He turned the stones to bread, He would know with certainty that He was the Son of God, and He could enter His public ministry assured of that fact.

But if He did, His identity and task would always be subject to His appetites. Each time He faced a difficult time He could say, "Hey, if I'm the Son of God, I can satisfy this appetite." His focus could be diverted from His *purpose* to His *need* in an instant. When meeting someone else's need, the dinner bell would ring. So even though Jesus had not eaten for 40 days, it seems He determined that He would not let His appetite define His identity and circumvent His purpose.

Priceless or Worthless?

The Scriptures tell the story of another man who handled a similar problem quite differently. Jacob and Esau were twin brothers who could not be more dissimilar. They did not look alike, and they were driven by different forces. Jacob was a schemer and a manipulator. Esau was a hunter. Jacob preferred the house and the kitchen, but Esau loved to be outdoors. There was one other difference. Esau was born first. Not by much, mind you, but he was the firstborn nevertheless, and that role gave him position, privileges, and possessions far above Jacob's.

As the story goes, one day Esau returned from a long hunting expedition with an enormous appetite. Maybe Esau had grown accustomed to eating often, or perhaps his hunt brought in nothing. Either way, apparently he felt as if he was about to die from hunger.

Esau spotted Jacob cooking red stew, and he told Jacob to give him some of it. Jacob said, "Sell me your birthright now."

Esau responded by saying, "I'm about to die; of what use is a birthright to me?"

So Jacob made the deal then and there for Esau's birthright, and afterward Jacob gave Esau the lentil stew and bread. Esau ate and drank and then rose and left. The next verse in Scripture says, "Thus Esau despised his birthright."

When I read that story as a young man, I was a little skeptical. Esau was a hunter—surely he didn't think he was going to die of hunger. Esau had lived off the land his whole life. Couldn't he just kill something or pick something or chew on something? How could he be so hungry that he would sell his identity and position in the family? No one could be that hungry.

But I now realize that sometimes an appetite can be so strong that everything pales in comparison. A person can feel as if he will die unless he feeds it. In those moments nothing is more important or valuable than satisfying the roar of his appetite. It is the only voice he hears, the only feeling he has, and the only thing he sees.

I have a hereditary disease called celiac. I can't digest the gluten in wheat, barley, and rye, so if I eat gluten, it damages my intestine and affects my immune system. The symptoms vary from person to person, but when I eat food with gluten, my body responds the way yours would if you suffered from food poisoning. It's coming out, and it's coming out fast.

It probably sounds like my condition should be easy to work around—simply avoid gluten. But the day I was diagnosed I discovered it wouldn't be so easy. When I came home from the doctor's office I turned on the television, and commercial by commercial I began to realize that practically all food advertised on television had gluten. Anything with white flour, such as bread, pizza, hamburger buns, pasta, gravy, cake, donuts—even beer and certain ketchups—they all had gluten.

My family and I learned to avoid gluten when we cook. However, traveling is difficult because I can seldom eat the food on airplanes, in airports, or at many restaurants and banquets. Candidly, at times I was so hungry and frustrated that I said to myself, *This is ridiculous. I have to eat something.* So I grabbed the only food available—like a piece of pizza—and ate it. My thinking was that I needed food in order to keep working, so any food was better than no food.

Unfortunately, that was not true. Instead, *no* food was better than *that* food! If my body could have talked it probably would have said, "Are you insane! Do you despise me or what? Don't you value your health at all, or do you have so little regard for your body that you would sell it out for a piece of pizza?"

You Are What You Eat

Sometimes it *is* about food. An appetite for food or alcohol can be out of control, and that appetite slowly *eats us* instead of the other way around. But I think that more often Satan detours us—takes us off our path—by appetites other than food. Appetites like greed, the need to control, or lust. They serve as his magnetic rods to pull us off course.

For instance, you may be driven by money and possessions. Certain people are just naturally good with money, and making money can actually validate who God made them to be. But a talent can morph into an appetite. It happens when Satan takes something about a man with this talent and turns it on himself. It is such a subtle thing that the man seldom sees the appetite—he only sees the talent because what he is doing feels so natural to him. That was the sinister plot behind Jesus' first temptation. It was just food, and eating food is a very natural thing.

In the case of the man with a talent for making money, the talent is part of who he is. It is embedded in his intentionality. But it was not designed to be attached to the high-performance engine of an appetite. Consequently—without even realizing it—when his ability to make money becomes separated from his purpose and is fused into his appetite, he will be drawn away from his path in order to serve his appetite. He makes money to *prove* who he is, not *because* of who he is. The first one serves the man, the second one serves others. To get back to his path, this man may need to start giving money away the way a man in a sinking ship bails water—by the buckets. As someone once said, "He doesn't need to give until it hurts, he needs to give until it feels good."

Control is much more subtle. Control can appear as concern for your friend, wife, or children. The mother of control is pride, but she hides back in the shadows. Because control can seem sincere and benevolent, it acts as a mask to hide the hideous face of insecurity, which breeds the fraternal twins named distrust and defensiveness.

Control consumes your attention and pulls you away from the path God set out for you to follow. Instead, you are forced to play God in other people's lives. When that happens, your enemy is elated because *he* knows you are not God and that you cannot be God in anyone's life—including your own. The sinister nature of the appetites feeding control is that once you indulge them, you will need to prove who you are over and over and over again.

Control is the dark side of responsibility, which can make a man a wonderful husband, father, and friend. But somewhere it flips, and when it does a man sees everything differently.

Probably no animal is more dangerous than wounded pride. It is like a Kodiak bear that screams in pain as it turns on its hunters. Many times a man's pride—his self-image—is wounded in his youth, and he spends his life's energy charging up the hill in pursuit of his perceived attackers. By his actions he solicits more and more attacks, never having a chance to recover from the first shot. He dies alone and feared, never having avenged his wounded pride.

A Ferocious Appetite

As you can probably testify in your own life, appetites rise and fall in individuals. But certain appetites can dominate and define an era, taking root in the culture at large. For instance, an appetite for drugs consumed the 1960s, while the 1980s were seen as the decade of greed—evidenced by the line from the movie *Wall Street*: "Greed is good."

Today many men are being diverted by the appetite of lust. Because I truly believe that this appetite has taken root in our culture, I am compelled to explore both the appetite and what it desires to consume. I will try to do so carefully, responsibly, and honestly, and I pray that you will extend grace to me as I get personal with you.

Many men have stopped pursuing their quest because they ducked into the tavern of lust for a quick drink, but they have stayed for dinner. It is late in the night, the family is asleep, and they are at the bar of the Internet ordering porn off the menu on their computer. An appetizer has turned into a seven-course meal, and all the waitresses are there just for them.

Many factors that would otherwise help these good men keep this ferocious appetite in check have been set aside because the Internet makes the user feel anonymous. No one knows, and the food seems to be free. But the bill is coming...and the price of the meal is their future.

Simulacrum

My family really enjoys Disneyland. Each of my children likes a different area, but my favorite is Main Street USA. It's festive, clean, and friendly.

I remember the days when the Main Street Electrical Parade made its way down the street on the warm summer nights just before the fireworks were set off above the castle. Main Street USA is designed to make visitors nostalgic for the good old days when the downtown areas in small towns across America were festive, clean, and friendly.

But Main Street USA never existed, nor does it exist anywhere in the United States today. When Mr. Disney desired to emulate the small-town look and feel, he developed what he believed was a simulation of the ideal downtown experience. But in his book, *Simulacra and Simulation,* philosopher Jean Baudrillard argued that Disney actually built a simulacrum—a copy with no original.

Disney simulated a place that didn't exist with the intention of passing it off as the real. If you go to Disneyland you will discover that regardless of how great the downtown area of your hometown is, it is inferior to Main Street USA. The unreal Main Street USA has become more real than the real. More desirable. More pleasurable. A copy with no original that makes you feel nostalgic for the good old days. It causes you to reminisce about the way you thought things could be.

Porn is like that. It is more real than the real. When the bill comes at the tavern of lust, you will find that not only has it distracted, detoured, and perhaps disqualified you, but it has also corrupted your sense of what is real. Think about it. Unless you live next door to a porn star, no matter how big your computer screen and how high its resolution, the women on your screen are mere electronic images. Nothing else.

The porn made you feel good about yourself, and for a moment you were a stud in fantasyland. You may have even experienced fireworks over your castle. But in the end—just like Main Street USA—it was only a fantasy.

So you leave the world of porn and return to the world of flesh and blood, only to be reminded that your wife is not a porn star. She has moods and bad breath. Consequently, the fantasy seems better. The unreal has corrupted your real, and ultimately your real will be replaced by the unreal. The appetite of lust will own you. It will take your prowess and sexual drive and turn you into a baboon in a zoo, sitting in the corner of his simulated sanctuary watching the world go by as he uses his hand to shoot his seed all over his imaginary world.

Your Seed

In the ancient Hebrew culture, if a married man died before he was able to produce a child and he had a brother old enough to sire a child, then that brother was responsible to impregnate the dead man's wife. This ensured that his name would be passed down and that the widow had someone to care for her when she was older.

Scripture tells of a man named Onan who was responsible to produce offspring for his sister-in-law Tamar. But he knew any child he produced with her would carry his brother's name, so each time he would lie with her, he pulled out at the last moment. Some translations say that Onan *spilled his seed* on the ground. God saw this act as wicked, and Scripture says God put him to death.

I've heard people suggest that this indicates God sees masturbation as wicked. That is understandable, but I think we should look at the reference to *seed* before we examine the reference to *spilled*.

Seed is a very interesting characteristic of nature. Early American settlers brought seed considerable distances to ensure that they would have food to sustain them in the new land. The most ridiculous and shortsighted thing a farmer could do was to eat or sell his entire crop and not hold any seed back for replanting. That is the "Eat, drink, and be merry, for tomorrow we die" attitude. Instead, a reasonable man reserves a certain amount of seed for the proper season and sows it into a prepared field.

Seed in and of itself doesn't seem like much. It is generally small and without any particular beauty. Few people display an arrangement of seeds in their home or walk guests through a seed garden. But the seed is valued because it is the vehicle of life. It carries life from place to place, time to time, and generation to generation.

I remember reading a news story about a man selling the seed of his prizewinning bull for a hundred thousand dollars. Investors pay incredible sums of money to breed their mares with champion racehorses. Seed is valuable, and it is always attached to purpose. Onan was wicked because he rejected the purpose behind his seed, yet he continued to engage in the act that transmitted it. He scattered his seed on the ground, and it returned to dust before it had a chance to create the life it was intended to create.

The only purpose of porn is to stimulate lust, and the only purpose of lust is to incite self-pleasure. It serves no one else and yields nothing. Perhaps a case can be made for self-pleasure, but to me the tragedy of porn is the scattered seed. People are paying hundreds of thousands of dollars for the right to use the seed of a bull or a horse while quality men of championship lineage scatter their seed to the wind—or pay a prostitute to dispose of it. Do we despise who we are that much?

Today, porn is pumped into the finest homes in town through the Internet, and it delivers a quantity and quality of content unimaginable just ten years ago. Porn stars are no longer taboo in society, and porn is being normalized rather than marginalized for our kids. But once again, this isn't just about the food—the porn—it is about the appetite.

Infected with a Virus

I have been involved in media production and media studies for nearly 20 years with the past ten years being focused on media's effects on individuals, groups, and culture. Much of my work has been focused on the Internet. Research takes me deep into the bowels of the Web, and I wade through all kinds of content, technology, and systems to examine changes in the way content is produced and delivered. I also study the ways Web users interact with and navigate that content.

I recently began a research project that required me to look for cutting-edge Internet content delivery systems. This project took me in and through sites that used advanced tools to publish and track Web content. In the course of this study I inevitably encountered systems designed to push porn in front of Web users and then draw them through a maze of associated sites. As I tracked the ways the Web tools pushed content into the face of users and then pulled them in, I discovered a force attached to porn that went way beyond the images.

I was already well aware that porn was simply the bait that allowed the site to unleash viruses and spyware into users' computers, but suddenly I felt the same thing happening in me. Images not only infected my computer but also planted viruses and spyware in me. I could sense these viruses attempting to attach themselves to my natural appetite and turn that appetite against me. I clearly saw that my appetite—the mechanism designed to keep me alive by reminding me to eat—had been infected with a high-performance virus. It intended to turn my appetite onto myself and eat me alive. Suddenly, I was no longer the hunter—I was the hunted.

Left unchecked, the appetite of lust could distract me from my path. If it were to continue unimpeded it would disqualify me from the work I have spent substantial time, energy, and money pursuing, and then it would turn on my family and erode those relationships. An uncontrolled appetite would compromise my life path and the means by which I pursue my quest to be known.

When I recognized what was happening I did the only thing I could do. I ratted myself out. I didn't recognize Satan's attack as quickly as Jesus did in the wilderness, but when I did, I took my wife aside and said, "Honey, I'm under attack. I'm trying to do my work on the Internet, and a very strong force is trying to pull me in."

I looked her in the eye and continued, "It's like an insatiable appetite of lust. It's trying to control me and destroy me in the very thing I do for a living. You need to know about it."

I understand that not every man could tell his wife what I told mine. Only an incredible woman with the grace of God in her life could handle this kind of confession and not feel betrayed or lose trust in her husband. But for me, the worst thing I could do was hide my battle from her. I was determined that I would not be destroyed by a rogue appetite. And I knew that she would be my strongest ally.

After we talked, I told her that she and I both needed one other person to know about it. Otherwise, Satan could turn this attack into a dark unspoken secret that we tried to hide, which would put me back at square one. Hiding something means it is still there—it's just out of sight. But I also had to be very careful because I didn't want to share this kind of thing with a person without a long history of mutual trust. Some men may have many options, but for me the list is very short.

I called a very close friend who happens to be a priest. I said, "Victor, I am calling on you both as a friend and as a priest. I sense that I am being attacked by—for lack of a better term—an appetite of lust. I need you to pray for me as often as you remember to for a while."

I told him about the strong force I sensed and that I understood what was behind the appetite. I also told him I was committed to not giving in to it. It was my way of saying, "Get behind me, Satan. I won't get detoured, distracted, or disqualified by an appetite. I am on a quest to be known."

So if I was so careful about telling someone else, why am I telling you? This is a very public forum to tell such a private story. I have two reasons.

The first reason is that I recognize what happened to me as an attack, an attempt to distract and ultimately detour me from my path. It was an attack against my identity, and the fact of the matter is that I know who I truly am. I am not a person ruled by appetites, and certainly not this appetite. How do I know that? Because I believe it in my heart, and my wife and my friend Victor believe as well. I am not willing to trade my identity.

The second reason is that I believe a great number of men—the majority of men—to a greater or lesser degree struggle with this same thing. I may be wrong, and if I am, I am delighted to be so. But if I am right, then you may ·just need someone to reach down into your darkness and urge you to do whatever is necessary to push your chair back from the table, stand up, and walk away from that appetite. I couldn't ask you to do it if I didn't know what it takes and if I wasn't sure it could be done.

Aron Ralston is a world-class mountain climber. He has scaled the peaks of dozens of mountains and prevailed in incredibly difficult conditions. So he was optimistic and relaxed that sunny Saturday when he started out to hike and explore a desolate wilderness area of southern Utah.

Newspaper and television accounts of the events that transpired over the coming days explain that Aron was moving through a three-foot wide slot in one of the myriad canyons in the area when an 800-pound boulder shifted. When the enormous rock moved, it pinned Aron's right arm to the wall of the slot. At first, Aron was fairly optimistic about finding a way to release himself or perhaps being rescued. He tried to use ropes from his pack to move the boulder, and then he turned to chipping at the rock with a small knife. As the sun set and the temperature dropped, Aron began to come to grips with the serious nature of his predicament. He could not free himself, and rescue planes flying overhead would never be able to see him deep in the canyon.

Saturday turned to Sunday, which became Monday and then Tuesday, and still Aron had made no progress in his attempt to be free. Finally, he knew he had to turn the knife on himself.

But the knife was now dull from days of digging and scraping the hard rock, so he knew it could never cut through the bones of his forearm. As the light of day gave way to the darkness of Wednesday night, Aron became resigned to the fact that he would never be free of the weight that bound him. He had lived a life of extraordinary accomplishments, but now an uneventful recreational exercise had led him to what could only be called an unremarkable death.

Stirred Thursday morning by a dream during moments of fitful sleep, Aron found renewed determination to pursue one last, extreme option. Aron pushed his body as high as he could up the walls of the ravine and let go. As the weight of his body plunged to the ground he heard the upper bones in his right forearm snap.

Even with the excruciating pain, the fracture gave Aron hope, and he realized that if he could summon the will and push through the pain, he might be able to free himself. So he lowered himself down into the crevice as far as he could and then lunged up as quickly and forcefully as possible, hoping his body weight would provide the torque needed to break the lower bones in his forearm. Once again, he heard the crisp crack as the bones snapped in two.

Finally, using small tools in his pocket knife, Aron cut the muscles, tendons, and ultimately the nerve that connected his hand to the rest of his arm. His plan was radical, but he was free. Aron told former NBC News anchor Tom Brokaw that the escape was the most freeing moment of his life. He still had to repel down a 60-foot cliff and walk out of the canyon, but he was no longer trapped by the rock.

Refuse to Feed the Appetite

Jesus said, "If your right hand causes you to sin, cut it off." Aron recognized that he could either keep his right hand and die, or he could cut off his right hand and live. I'm not saying you need to cut your hand off, but maybe you need to cut off your home Internet connection. Maybe you need to get blocking software and give your wife the password. And as you cut off an unhealthy appetite, find a better alternative. For me, drinking hot water replaced drinking coffee. I enjoyed having the cup in my hand, but I was free from the controlling appetite. Putting something new in your hand may open doors you could never have imagined.

You may not have a priest or be able to talk to your wife. You don't need to do what I did or what Aron did. But if you are struggling with appetites, you must cut them off, or they will drag you to the grave.

You may seem to be fine because you've been indulging your appetite for some time, and nothing has happened yet. And nothing may happen for a while. But when you leave your life's path to pursue something that catches your attention, you don't always see the danger that awaits you.

Sidetracked

For seven years, two men spent the last week of September reliving frontier life in the same meadow in the foothills of the Appalachians. Authentic down to their long underwear, they lived off what they could scavenge, pick, or hunt. The replica muzzle-loaded flint rifles were heavier and clumsier than the bolt-action rifles they used the rest of the year, but they added to the challenge. For one week every year, these men lived in Virginia as if the year were 1746.

One morning after finishing breakfast by the fire in front of the same one-room cabin they always rented, they headed down the trail to find game for dinner. As they passed a narrow, dry stream bed, they caught a glimpse of what looked like a small black bear entering the woods from the stream bed on their right. The men had no intention of shooting the bear, but one of them decided he would try to get a closer look. So as his friend stopped to roll a cigarette using tobacco leaves they cured from last year's trip, he slung his rifle over his shoulder and stepped toward the heavy brush next to the path.

As the man slowly made his way toward the place the bear entered the woods, he had no idea that when he slung his rifle over his shoulder, the butt of the gun knocked the nozzle cover off his horn of gunpowder. From the time he stepped away from the path until he knelt down 20 feet later to watch the bear digging in a rotted-out stump, a steady stream of gunpowder had been following his every move.

The man held his first two fingers toward his eyes and then pointed toward the woods, indicating to his friend back on the path that he had spotted the bear. The man on the path nodded and pulled the cigarette he had just rolled toward his lips with his left hand and used the thumbnail on his other hand to strike the wooden match in his hand.

As fire leaped from the head of the match, the man on the path caught sight of the charcoal gray thread of gunpowder winding from just beyond his right foot into the dry riverbed. In one move he spit the homemade cigarette from his lips and shoved the match into his mouth. His tongue felt the sting of the hot match, but its moisture extinguished the fire. He motioned for the man down by the bear's path to step back, but the man looked annoyed and moved his hands with intensity in a sweeping "come here" motion.

Finally, the man on the path yelled out, "Hey, I don't care about the bear. You've got a line of gunpowder running straight to your back, and I nearly threw a match on it. Now get out of there!"

If I may be so bold, let me be your friend on the path. Get out of there! I say that with an intensity that I cannot convey in writing. And I say it with intensity because I know I'm not the only one who sees it. Your enemy sees it. And he is just waiting for the perfect time to lay his match to your trail of gunpowder. It may be while you are distracted by appetites. It may be when you have failed or when you are discouraged. Or he may wait and use the trail to follow you to a pivotal moment in your quest, at which time he will do what he always does. He will ambush you.

You may not immediately relate to the two men, but the chances are very good that you have a trail of gunpowder behind you. You must go back and remove sections in the line of powder so that if one section is ignited, it will burn out before causing any harm.

Try going back to where it all began. Whether your issue is lust, greed, or wounded pride, consider going to a quiet place for an afternoon. Try to remember the first time you had a strong feeling of lust or the first time you felt your self-image was attacked. The lust probably happened in a very innocent time, and your pride was probably wounded in a happy or peaceful time. The event had such an effect on you because you had not yet put up your defenses or dealt with anything like what happened. Take a pen and paper with you and briefly restate the event. This is just for you, so what you write only has to make sense to you.

Continue to recall each time you remember something like this happening throughout your life. As you recall these events, you may find that something happened before the one you thought was first. Don't worry about ordering the list until you are done.

You'll find that this is not a difficult exercise. Each of the events you list are key frames in your selective memory. You don't remember everything that happens in your life, but you remember certain things for a reason, and most often they link with and reinforce other memories of lust or hurt. Give yourself about an hour or so to sit, think, and identify these memories.

Once you feel that the list is pretty complete, go back to the first one and pray. Ask God to forgive you for engaging in that specific event or entertaining that thought and to put a wall of protection around you from that point on. If another person is involved or if someone wounded your pride, forgive them by name out loud. State his name, clearly state what he did to you, and then forgive him.

The purpose of this exercise is to remove the powder of that event, to enable a God who is not limited by time and space to heal and protect you at that specific point, and to release you from whatever is keeping you from God's path for your life.

6

THE HOUSE

Blessed is the man
who walks not in the counsel of the wicked,
nor stands in the way of sinners,
nor sits in the seat of scoffers;
but his delight is in the law of the LORD,
and on his law he meditates day and night.
He is like a tree
planted by streams of water
that yields its fruit in season,
and its leaf does not wither.

PSALM 1:1-3

....

SUNJIT KUMAR WAS JUST A BOY when his parents died. He was sent to live with his grandfather, who didn't have the time or the inclination to take care of him. Sunjit's grandfather locked the young boy in a chicken coop near his house on a small island in Fiji, where for several years Sunjit spent every moment of every day alone with the chickens. When he was 12 years old, he finally escaped and found his way to a local hospital.

But the hospital staff had no idea what to do with Sunjit because after years of living with chickens he had taken on the characteristics and mannerisms of a chicken. After a few feeble attempts to treat him, they confined him to a room, where they watched him perch himself on the end of the bed like a chicken roosting. Sunjit would hop around the room like a chicken and peck at his food as if he had a beak. He constantly held his hands in a chicken-like fashion and made noises that resembled chicken calls. Sunjit's behavior was so bizarre that the hospital staff often tied him to the bed.

Twenty years later, in 2004, a woman named Elizabeth Clayton discovered 32-year-old Sunjit in the small hospital room he had lived in all those years. Elizabeth persuaded a team of doctors to examine Sunjit, and after a broad range of tests, they all agreed he had no mental defects or anything physically wrong. Sunjit had simply become a chicken. That was his world and the way he saw himself.

Who Are You?

Very few of us see ourselves as a chicken, but let me ask you this question: Who *are* you? Perhaps I should ask the question this way: Who have you become?

Sunjit wasn't born a chicken, but by the time he was 32 years old he (and everyone else) was convinced that he was a chicken. When people looked at him, they saw a chicken. When he looked at himself, he saw a chicken. This self-image drove all Sunjit's actions, and these actions reinforced the chicken-boy image of Sunjit in others, which they then projected back onto him.

The self-image and the projected image are like the two electronic eyes that control an automatic garage door opener. These optical devices maintain a single beam of light between them and instantaneously reinforce that image back and forth. They look at each other and see themselves. Our self-image constructs itself from both its projection and the reflection it receives from others, and it learns to adjust itself to maintain a clear image—similar to the way electronic eyes are periodically adjusted.

So again I ask, who have you become? Are you pleased with the man you are? If today you saw your body lying in a casket at the front of a church, would you honestly be able to say you became the man God made you to be?

If you are like most men the answer is at least a qualified no. Instead, we look in the mirror every morning and stare at the man we've become, quietly wondering where the man we truly are has gone.

Unfortunately, in most cases the man you really are will waste away in an arid, desolate, and ephemeral region of your being unless you "break the beam." Like breaking the beam of a garage door opener, you will need to stop the existing signal between the self-image and the projected/reflected image. You must do this before the door of life closes for you.

What does that mean? Simply, you must rediscover the man God created you to be. The good news is that He provided the means for you to do so, and He integrated—or preprogrammed—the ability to do it into your life and into the life of every single person around you. Why should you die never having really lived? Why not live so that you will never die?

In broad terms, the key to unlocking the man you were made to be is this: Know and be known. But remember, one doesn't work without the other. You can't know without being known any more than you can amputate one of your legs and expect to walk your path. The left leg advances and then carries the weight of your body while the right leg advances. This process continues instinctively.

So how do you really know yourself, and how does being known by others enable you to know yourself? Truthfully, the process is at once complex and simple. It is grueling and painful while at the same time liberating and satisfying. And it is the left-right-left pattern of life. When it becomes instinctive to you, you will begin to see the same process in others, which will empower you as a husband, father, friend, and leader.

Start where you are today. This chapter will help you discover how you became the man you are so you can determine your authenticity. If necessary we will break the beam, stop the door, and adjust the electronic eyes. Then, in the following chapters, we will move forward and chart a course for life. You will adjust your aim away from the wrong target and set your sights on the real target. And in time, you will hit the mark.

The Foundation

To a large degree, certain other people shape you into the person you become. That is the process of being known. But this process does not mean that others decide who you are. Instead, others help you discover the person

God made you to be. God laid the foundation of your life, and He placed intentionality in you.

Think of the way a house is constructed. Carpenters, masons, electricians, and other craftsmen work together to build a home. Yet they don't just show up one morning and indiscriminately start framing and wiring a house according to their moods or their opinion of how the house should be built.

Months—and sometimes years—before the laborers arrive, the architect designs the house. Then, before any part of the house is erected, a foundation is laid. Laborers don't start building a house without a foundation. Neither do they build a five-bedroom ranch-style house on a two-bedroom townhouse foundation. Instead, tradesmen and craftsmen wait until the foundation is poured according to the architect's plans, and then they build on that foundation.

God the Architect imagined the best you, and He laid a foundation to fit that plan. God didn't just imagine how nice it would be if you turned out a certain way. His intention—His design—was carried forward when He laid the foundation of your life.

My wife had her eye on five acres of land for sale close to where we live. We were not in a position to buy it, so Lisa watched with a touch of envy when the new owner began to construct his new home. For months she saw very little activity other than the occasional surveyor and the running of utilities. Finally, tractors appeared, and the land around the crest of the hill began to be shaped and molded.

We passed the property each day to and from home. Sometimes the lot was buzzing with workers, and sometimes nothing seemed to happen at all. During the quiet times we speculated all kinds of things—maybe the builders ran out of money or the architectural plans changed or the project was abandoned. But eventually the framing began, and a house began to take shape.

A sign at the front of the lot indicated that the future home owner hired a contractor known for building incredible homes. Over a period of months, certain features of the house emerged. It would have three levels, six garages, and a stately stone exterior. After months of work on the exterior during the summer and fall, the weather changed, and construction moved to the inside.

Expert designers coordinated the interior color scheme, the furniture, the artwork, the home theater system, and the myriad other details. Because the interior had significant custom woodwork, it required more than six months to be completed. But when the house was finished, it was a magnificent structure.

The owners hosted an open house. People from all over our small community streamed through the doors and admired the beauty, the attention to detail, and the high-tech features. I stood in the foyer and sipped coffee as I listened to remarks neighbors made coming and going. I heard dozens of comments about the exterior, the landscaping, the pool and decking, the entertainment system, the kitchen, the office, and the veranda.

Just imagine for a moment that the architect decided to attend the open house. Can you picture him walking up the steps and through the open doors and saying, "Hey, what an interesting place to put the dining room!" Do you think he would walk down the hall and into the kitchen and be amazed at the way the kitchen and family room flowed together so well? Sure, he might make a remark about the artwork or maybe the choice of colors used to accent the angles and arches that make up the three-story entryway. But one of the least surprised people to attend the open house would be the architect.

As I stood in the foyer of that newly built home during the open house and listened, I did not hear one comment about the foundation. No one mentioned the architect. Nevertheless, nothing directed the shape, characteristics, and uniqueness of the house more than the design and the foundation.

Jesus knew that you would face decisions about where and how to build your life, and He spoke about the importance of the foundation. In our day, Jesus would have said that the wise man studies the blueprints, seeks advice, and submits his agenda to the architect's plan. When he builds the house of his life, he builds it on the foundation. Then, when the rain, wind, and floods come—as they inevitably will—the house will stand.

The fool gives little thought to his foundation. The fool makes the decision about where to build his life based on the sound of the powerful surf, the smell of salted air, and the sight of the sunbathing bodies. He chooses to build his house on sand. Like homes built on certain unstable hillsides along the

California coastline, when the rain, wind, and floods come—as they inevitably will—the house will fall, and great will be its destruction.

People build homes in many different styles and most of us prefer a certain look and feel. A friend of mine built a home on a hill in an exclusive area of town, blending the look and feel of a Cape Cod home with a Californian stylishness. It was a unique home among other unique homes, and it combined his taste with that of his wife. Homes can be brick, stucco, or wood, whichever fits the taste and style of the owners, provided they are built on a foundation.

In a similar way, the house of your life can be personalized several different ways. You could have chosen from several different options in life—to attend an in-state college or one out of state, or to focus on basketball rather than football. Just like the choices of interior colors, furnishings, and artwork, the house of your life will reflect decisions and choices you made during construction.

Yet, your life-house should still be built on the foundation and according to the blueprints. If you put a dining room in the place where the architect had the builders plumb a bathroom, the room will never feel right. It will be small. Guests who instinctively search for the bathroom may inadvertently find themselves in the dining room. Perhaps the sink could function as a wet bar and the shower enclosure could be modified into a china cabinet, but the room will never have that natural, comfortable feel. It will seem out of sorts.

You can make choices that compliment the design God has for your life, or you can make decisions that will keep you from ever feeling natural or comfortable. If you set a dining table on a bathtub, you can decorate it all you want, but the bathtub is still the bathtub. You can try your whole life to do or be something God never intended for you, and you will never be more than a B player in those areas. That may be life, but that isn't living. So let's go back and see how you got here in order to get a better idea of how your life conforms to God's design.

Ideally Constructed

How did Sunjit Kumar, born with no mental or physical defects, grow up to be a chicken? The same way a young man named Abe, born into abject poverty, grew up to be president of the United States of America. Both men constructed their lives.

A child's world is usually very small, and a great deal of his time is spent at home with family members. These people help him craft his image of himself, and they usually have a strong emotional attachment to the child. They have big dreams for his future. The amount of time Mom and Dad devote to this process in the early years makes their roles as image-designers so very determinative.

Your parents told you who you are. When you were young, they seemed to know more about you than you knew about yourself. Week by week, month by month, and year by year they helped you frame the walls and attach the beams of the house that would be you. They did this by their words. They did this by their expressions. They did this by their silence.

But they didn't make it up. They may have recognized that God laid a foundation for your life and that He designed you to be a particular man. Their instincts should have been to watch you from the day you were born to look for clues about who you are. They probably anticipated many things about you because of your lineage. As the saying goes, "The apple doesn't fall far from the tree, but neither does it fall from a peach tree." Apple trees produce apples, and your parents' DNA will produce a son with some of their own characteristics. You may have your father's eyes or your uncle's ears. You may be athletic like your grandfather or analytical like your mother.

But your parents probably also looked for unique qualities in you, things beyond your ears and eyes. They patiently probed for characteristics that would begin to reveal your talents and temperament—the direction you may go. As you grew, they began to call out the traits they perceived, and you used those words to build your self-image. We can even see this pattern in Scripture where it says, "Train up a child in the way he should go, and when he is old (under other outside influences) he will not depart from it."

Although memories stored in a child's mind during his first few years may not be accessible later in life, they set the broad tones that tint most future interactions. Early memories of home form the color palate of life. These shades and hues incline the young boy to see his world—and his place in it—as either warm, welcoming, and peaceful, or cold, harsh, and unforgiving.

With an unconscious symmetry, your mother and father worked together to construct the general framework of your life on God's foundation. Their work erected walls that closed some things out. But the walls also defined rooms that were otherwise merely indeterminate space. Similar to a pair of birds building a nest, your parents played specific, complementing roles in framing, defining, and coloring the rooms in your life-house.

Your mother gave you a sense of place. She was a fire in the fireplace that made your living room feel warm and peaceful. The fire provided the light you needed to read God's blueprints, and it cooked the food that kept you emotionally fed. The fire was always glowing. The best place in the world was home.

Meanwhile, your father was at work on the outside of your house. He protected you when the house was a skeletal structure—wide-open and vulnerable to the world. Before your front door was in place, he stood in the doorway so that you could feel secure when sleeping by the fireplace at night.

But he also roused you out of bed in the morning and helped you understand the concept of work. "The house won't build itself," he said. He taught you responsibility, dependability, honesty, and self-sacrifice.

Dad offset your desire to remain comfortably inside your life-house. He sparked your curiosity to explore the neighborhood. He provoked you to venture out. He made you aware that one day you would need to prepare to move both your life-house and your fire down the street.

Our Construction Experience

Does this process describe your home experience as a child? Perhaps it does, but for many it does not. Parents who are wise builders are a blessing, but most parents were still trying to discover who *they* were at the same time we needed them to tell us who *we* are. Too many times they simply tried to keep us from inheriting their dark side. Yet in a strange twist, their words, facial expressions, and silence often directed us toward the very image our parents tried to avoid.

When my middle daughter was five years old and was first learning to ride a bicycle, we lived in graduate student housing. Four two-story buildings in our area created a small courtyard about 80 feet long and 40 feet wide with a sidewalk around the perimeter and grass in the middle. Nothing was in the grassy area other than a tree near the center and a small green utility box—about six inches square and two feet high—in the corner farthest from our building, about two feet inside the sidewalk.

My daughter had learned to balance herself on the bicycle for short distances, but she was still very wobbly and barely in control. On this particular day we decided that she should attempt to ride her bike around the courtyard—a route that required turns. So my wife and I instructed her to stay on the sidewalk and to be sure to watch out for that one small utility post in the far corner.

With a small push she set out on her bicycling adventure, rode up the long right side of the courtyard, and successfully navigated the left turn at the top of the courtyard. We yelled out words of encouragement as she continued across the top and around the second left turn onto the long sidewalk on the left side of the courtyard. As she rounded that corner and started back, she began to wobble, rode off the sidewalk to the left, and entered the grassy area. As if her bike were a big piece of steel and the utility post a powerful magnet, she rode the bicycle straight into the green utility post. It was the only obstacle in the courtyard but also the only thing I brought to her attention. I often wonder if she would have hit it if I hadn't mentioned it was there.

Our parents and siblings often spoke words they never intended for us to use as building blocks as we constructed our self-image. We interpreted their words of caution as descriptive words, and we used them to define ourselves. Other times they spoke carelessly or with sarcasm. But however the words were intended, we used them one by one to systematically build our life-house and figure out who we were in relationship to the rest of the world.

We don't know what kind of relationship Sunjit had with his parents. They may have done a great job helping Sunjit build his self-image on his foundation. His grandfather may have had no resources and may have even believed he was doing the best he could for the boy when he placed him in the chicken coop. But intentional or not, the grandfather's words and actions had considerable influence on the young boy.

Interestingly, at the age of 12, Sunjit rejected that image and escaped the world of the chickens. He ran away from his grandfather and sought someone—anyone—who would tell him who he was. Someone who could confirm or reject his identity as a chicken. His journey took him to a logical place—a hospital. Unfortunately, the professionals could not see past his behavior. They never caught a glimpse of the man God made Sunjit to be and instead focused on a misconstructed image that Sunjit could not shake.

Often, well-meaning people did the same thing to us when we were young. Doctors, pastors, and teachers could not get past malformed images to see who we were, so they reinforced a self-image we were trying to escape. They were the garage door eyes that both reflected and projected the "chicken boy" image we had of ourselves, so we resigned ourselves to it. When finally we reluctantly took ownership of that image, we may have escaped from a coop to a hospital room, but we were just as confined.

On a warm, sunny September morning, my friend Will and I hurried across the field behind our houses and into the doors of Lucille O'Neal Elementary School. It was the first day of school, and we were among the first students to arrive. We nearly ran down the hall as we checked the sheets of paper stapled on the doorpost of each classroom listing the students in that particular class that year. We discovered both of our names on one list and were thrilled to be in the same class. As we glanced back down the hallway, we spotted our new teacher walking toward us.

Full of excitement for the first day of school and at being placed in the same classroom, we both ran up to her with huge smiles on our face and exclaimed, "Mrs. _____, we're in your class!"

The words had barely left our lips before our new teacher squared up to us and—with one hand on her waist and the index finger of the other pointing at us and wagging up and down—said with a frowning face and snarling tone, "I know you are, boys, and so help me, if you give me any trouble, I'm going to come down on you so hard..." Her voice trailed off and we could only imagine what horrors might lay in store for disobedient boys.

My excitement was instantly replaced with fear and embarrassment. I wanted to disappear or apologize for existing. I had no idea what I had done the previous year to construct the image of some sort of troublemaker. I didn't recall being sent to the principal's office or being a problem for my teacher, but my new teacher obviously was not at all happy that I was in her classroom. I had been judged and found guilty even before I had arrived at school on that first day. Whatever else the year held, I could expect myself to be in trouble, and I was.

That one quick encounter, which couldn't have lasted more than five or six seconds, defined me for the next 15 years. It caused me to see myself in a way I had never seen myself before. It solicited behavior that reified the structure of that image, and I was in college before I recognized the way it had shaped me. I'm sure that before that day in the hallway of my elementary school, other words were spoken to me and other comments made about me that helped form the image of a troublemaker, but it was that piece of drywall from my teacher that brought the other pieces together into a definable area of my life-house.

Blessed Is the Man

Parents and authority figures aren't the only ones who shape us—so do brothers, sisters, and friends. Most of us recognize the degree to which friends influence our self-image, which in turn affects and motivates our actions and behavior. We then reinforce our self-image by monitoring other people's perception of our behavior and accepting or rejecting their assessment. So, as the saying goes, "Choose your friends wisely."

The verses at the beginning of this chapter stated that the righteous do not walk the path of the wicked scoffers, the people who aimlessly roam through life. The righteous avoid the women who draw them down a path to nowhere and the men who always look for the angle. They seek people who can be streams of water for them, and they plant themselves next to them. They look for men who refresh and challenge them and for women who help them to bear fruit in each season of life.

Self-esteem, a popular subject in our culture and schools, is largely shaped by the esteem we receive from others. Esteem is associated with the concepts of high regard, respect, and admiration. In other words, your opinion of yourself is significantly correlated with the opinion others have of you. Yet interestingly, as you get older you will give much greater weight to the opinions of people whom you believe truly know you. A remark by an elementary school teacher—good or bad—may drastically impact you, but you may blow off the same comment by a college professor.

Although this defense mechanism helps us as adults, it works against us when we receive compliments. When a person we don't know particularly well makes a favorable remark about us, we can think, *Well, they only think that because they don't know me. If they really knew me…*

In mere moments our delight at the kind words vanishes into the black hole of self-doubt, and we settle back into the person we've become. The hearth has no fire. The warmth is gone. The shifting shadows of resignation are then only occasionally broken up by a sudden burst of the harsh light of expectation.

The Remodel

Think back to how you saw yourself as a child. Who were you in the home? Who were your friends? These things formed the brick and mortar of the self-image you constructed. Perhaps now you can go back to the blueprints and determine whether your house was built to code. Did you build your life-house on the foundation?

As you honestly move through this process, you may discover that you used a lot of flawed or defective material. By that I mean you may have taken shortcuts, developed habits, or pursued friendships with little thought to the long-term consequences.

Whether you were meticulous or sloppy in your building methods, you have now spent a considerable amount of time living in the house you built. Had you realized the long-term effects of your choices, you may have done things differently.

Did you erect walls that artificially separated you from the real you? Could it be that you built rooms of your life-house with sentences about yourself that may have seemed true at the time but were not? Even today these sentences keep you from being the person you really are or doing the things you were made to do.

Perhaps you were told you had no athletic ability, or you were bad at math, or you were untrustworthy. When you heard those words, you may have felt the sting of disappointment because you had always felt you had that particular ability, or you believed you had good character. Still, you have worn those labels and used those sentences to describe yourself for so long now that you accept them as fact. But those facts may not be true.

Several years ago I attended a lecture by the late distinguished professor and author Neil Postman. He began by telling a story about a research project involving fish. Dr. Postman noted that carp love to eat minnows. That fact is well established. When the researchers dropped several hundred minnows into a tank filled with carp, the minnows were gone, in mere minutes—gleefully consumed by the carp as the two groups swam together throughout the tank.

A short time after the minnows were gone researchers maneuvered all the carp to one side of the tank and installed a Plexiglas panel that divided the tank into two chambers. The division wasn't apparent from the carp's point of view. Then hundreds of minnows were dropped into the side of the tank opposite the carp.

Once again the carp pursued the minnows, only to hit the transparent divider. This happened time after time as the carp saw their favorite food—minnows—but could not get to them. With sore lips and empty stomachs the carp now had a new sentence to add to their personal database. To the first carp descriptor—carp love to eat minnows—must be added the second qualifier—minnows are not available. After a while, researchers quietly removed the divider, allowing the carp to swim together with the minnows.

Amazingly, the carp swam right by the minnows and never seemed to even *try* to eat one. Day after day the carp and minnows swam side by side and all around each other with the same result. Not a single carp ate a single minnow. Why? Because the carp believed the minnows were not available. With no other food, the carp ultimately began to die from starvation. Although carp love to eat minnows, and minnows were there for the taking, the carp had become convinced that minnows are not available.

The second sentence may have once been true: *Minnows were not available.* An artificial wall was interjected into the life-tank of the carp, causing a carp to see his world differently from the way he had seen it before. But the existence of this imperceptible wall did not change the fundamental fact that *carp love to eat minnows.* That fact remained ingrained in the nature of the carp. Yet when the wall was removed and the minnows were once again available for food, the carp unconsciously chose to die rather than to reexamine the sentences that defined their lives.

What sentences define your life? If I were to ask you to tell me who you are, what would you say? How much time would you spend telling me who you are not?

You may never have been told who you are. Perhaps no one took the time to draw out the traits and character God placed in you. The fire in your fireplace gave you no warmth. Your father may have been so busy guarding the door and extending his life into the village of life that he never got around to inviting you outside and helping you discover your place in the community. So now, while you march through the days of your life, you are quietly looking around, hoping to stumble across the man you were made to be.

Or do you feel you were misconstructed? Perhaps you sense that your life-house was built askew of its foundation or that an unexpected storm of life damaged your structure before it was protected. Storms of divorce, disease, and poverty can cause us to distance ourselves from the process of building our life-house or even abandon it.

In the movie *Hidalgo*, viewers are initially led to believe that the lead actor was nicknamed Far Rider because of his legacy as a long-distance, endurance horseman in the old West. But deeper into the movie, an elderly Indian tells the protagonist he is named Far Rider because he rides far from himself and never looks toward home. Do you ever find yourself doing the same thing— riding far from yourself? Do you distance yourself from your home?

So often we just accept the damaged structure as it is and conclude that our life-house is the best we can do, considering our circumstances. Inside ourselves we dutifully live our lives neutered, docile, and passive. Or we mull and fume while we put on a happy face and say, "It's all good."

But do we ever really stop to consider the fact that the foundation is still solid? It remains intact. All we need to do is decide to assemble the resources and dedicate the time to do a remodel.

Fighting Against Ourselves

The story of Jacob in the Scriptures describes a tormented man. His parents named him Jacob, which meant *schemer*. His mom tutored him in schemeology, while his father ignored him. Jacob spent a good deal of his early life—up through what we would call middle-age—running from his name and the decisions he made as the result of his constructed image. But Jacob determined that he would return home. He would face himself and the family he deceived in the hope of reclaiming his true identity and inheritance.

Jacob began in a tangible way. He pulled up his stakes, gathered his family and possessions, and headed toward home. He sent representatives ahead of him to distribute gifts and tell his story. He didn't position himself as a triumphant prodigal but as a humble fellow servant and family member. All this work and effort was admirable and appropriate, but it was all preparatory. To reclaim his identity he would have to venture past the visible structure of his life-house and go to its foundation. He had to go back to the blueprints. The change had to begin at the deepest level.

As Jacob approached his native land, he perceived what can only be described as a holy area—a window to heaven and a window in time. So as evening drew near, Jacob sent his family and possessions ahead while he remained behind all alone with God. Scripture indicates that at that point and at that place Jacob somehow wrestled with God. But what really happened there?

That passage of Scripture actually says that a man wrestled with Jacob, and then just a few verses later it seems to suggest that Jacob was really wrestling with God. As the story progresses we see that this was a pivotal moment for Jacob, yet the Bible describes the event in just a few verses. I've given this some thought, so with full disclosure that this is just my opinion, I'd like to tell you what I think happened. But first let me give you a little history.

Many years earlier, at his mother's urging, Jacob had deceived his father, Isaac, and received the blessing meant for his older brother, Esau. Jacob had already used Esau's appetite against him to gain his birthright, but Isaac's blessing was highly valued. Most often the father's blessing was conveyed when the child was moving into maturity and considered an adult.

The father would reflect on his entire life experience with his son—from the moment his son was born to the point of adulthood—and form a composite of his son's identity. This process would be similar to saying, "My son, I have watched you your entire life, and it is clear to me that this is who you are—the good and the bad of it."

But as valuable as that was, the father did not stop there. He then drew from those perceptions to define the son's destiny. He went from *this is who you are* to *this is who you will be.* Can you imagine how powerful an experience like that would be?

Well, Isaac was not particularly fond of Jacob, mostly because they were so very different. Jacob knew that full well, and he was probably pretty sure Isaac's blessing for him would not be particularly inspiring. Can you imagine how devastating an experience like that would be?

So Jacob and his mother determined they would steal a future. So Jacob deceived his father Isaac into thinking he was Esau, and consequently Isaac spoke powerful words of a great destiny over and into Jacob. Wow! Now Jacob had a direction. He may not have had Esau's characteristics, but he had the key to Esau's future. His father had just spoken Esau's full personal profile directly into Jacob.

When Esau found out, he was livid. He stormed into Isaac's tent and demanded the blessing due him. However, his father indicated that as much as he would love to be able to, he could not retract the words he spoke over Jacob. Nor could he speak those same words to Esau. In his understandable rage, Esau determined to kill his brother. So in short order, Jacob fled with Esau's identity.

We see a picture of that story today when a person's identity is stolen. A man's name is associated with a credit profile he worked his entire life to build. He has plans for the future based on his history. But suddenly his name is hijacked and used by someone else to buy a future that person did not earn.

So in Jacob's case, this is what I believe could have happened. Jacob seems to have spent years trying to validate who he was, all the while riding farther and farther from himself. He worked hard and consistently tried to do the right thing. He was diligent and successful, but somewhere deep inside I think he was trying to *prove* himself rather than *be* himself.

And so God orchestrated circumstances that would lead Jacob to return home to face himself. I don't think Jacob really knew where that process would lead, but I suspect that his thoughts were to apologize, to pay restitution through gifts, and ultimately to *defend* his life and who he had become. He would humbly confess and say he was sorry.

So as Jacob was about to nod off to sleep, perhaps he was thinking one of two things would happen the next day. Best case—Esau would accept his apology and give him a chance to defend his life. Worst case—Esau would once again reject Jacob and seize his family and life work. Jacob would start again from scratch to build an identity.

But as Jacob fell asleep a man began to wrestle with him. Who was this man? On one level, I think it was Jacob himself. The true Jacob—the Jacob that God made—wanted to come alive. God caused circumstances to occur that led Jacob back to a place where *The Man God Made Jacob to Be* would once again have a chance to emerge—to take control and fulfill his destiny.

But this wasn't the way Jacob wanted it to happen. He wanted to *defend* who he had become. He felt compelled to explain how tough his life had been and how he had fought through so much to become who he was. This was all true. His life *had* been tough—so much so that the Jacob who lay down to sleep would not give up. He would not let *The Man God Made Jacob to Be* win.

As the new day broke, signaling the end of the struggle, *The Man God Made Jacob to Be* started to leave. As he did, Jacob suddenly realized that in fighting *The Man God Made Jacob to Be,* he was actually fighting God. This was God's best for him, and he was fighting it. God would not force Himself on Jacob.

In a flash, Jacob reached out as if to grab both God and *The Man God Made Jacob to Be* and said something like this: "Wait…I realize what is happening, and I cannot let You go. You want to tell me who I am, You brought me to this place in my life, and I have been fighting You."

Jacob continued, "Please…bless me. You are my father. You made me and have watched me develop to this point. Bless me…tell me who I am."

God—in the form of the man—said, "Tell me your name. Stop defending yourself or blaming others and admit to me who you have become."

Just as the name on the credit report details the financial transactions of our lives, God helped Jacob see that how he was known—his name—detailed who he had become. At that point God said, "You are no longer Jacob the swindler and cheat. You are Israel." The name Israel can mean either *Strives with God* or *God Strives*.

Then God touched Jacob at the hip socket. This became a physical sign that would always reflect a spiritual change. The new Jacob—Israel—would have a limp as a reminder that he wrestled both *The Man God Made Jacob to Be* and God, and Jacob is finally released to live.

Chicken-Boy

When chicken-boy Sunjit finally met Elizabeth, he was reunited with Sunjit the human being. His nature was restored. Newspaper reports indicate that in the short time Elizabeth has worked with Sunjit he has made remarkable progress. He speaks and is learning to read.

What changed? Sunjit met a person who recognized who he was. That person called him out, and that process caused others to know the real Sunjit.

Sunjit came alive because he was finally known. Jacob came alive because he was finally known. Do you want to finally live before the light of eternity arrives, signaling the end of God's struggle to know you and your quest to know yourself? It's time to wrestle. Let's get ready to rumble!

7

THE FIRE

Your identity is your most valuable possession.
Protect it!
MRS. INCREDIBLE, FROM
THE ANIMATED MOTION PICTURE *THE INCREDIBLES.*

....

IN THE LATE WINTER of my sophomore year of high school I had a dream. In the dream I rode a bus to school, walked inside, and went to my locker. After turning the combination and opening the locker door, I reached up to take off my winter coat. That's when I realized I had nothing on but my underwear.

I quickly glanced to each side, checking the hall to see how many people were looking and laughing while I simultaneously covered myself with my arms and tried to squeeze into the locker. Amazingly, no one had noticed... yet. My four-year high school only had about 400 kids, but the one L-shaped hall was really crowded. Though I knew it would be tough, I realized I had to get home without being discovered.

Somehow I managed to make it down the hall, out the door, and through the parking lot without anyone seeing me. But I had seven miles of country road and rural town to traverse before I could get home, and with practically no clothing to keep me warm that cold, wintry morning, the journey seemed impossible. I recall that in the last part of the dream I was snaking down a dry ditch on the side of the road, trying to avoid detection by the passing cars. I can still remember thinking in my dream that I was never going to make it home without being exposed.

Nakedness

I'm sure a psychotherapist would say my dream revealed all sorts of personality quirks besides the normal adolescent angst of high school. But I think most of us struggle to some degree with the fear of being discovered. Maybe I should say *uncovered*. For that reason alone, the idea that we are each on a quest to be known would seem contradictory at best and maybe even bordering on nonsensical. But the fear of being uncovered is rooted in the fear of rejection, which we know by thoughts like these: *Any day now, they are going to figure out I have no idea what I'm doing*, or *If you really knew me, you wouldn't like me.*

Somewhere back in time we each jumped on the bus of life and rode to school, where we suddenly realized we were naked. Since then we have been trying to get back home through the trenches of life. But the deep sense of dread inside tells us we will never make it to the end without being uncovered.

But where did this feeing of nakedness originate? When did we sense that we were naked and begin to fear that someone might expose us? Although we tend to think we were the first ones to see our nakedness, we probably didn't know we were naked until someone told us so. That happened either by words, a gaze of the eyes, or some sort of action that made us aware of our own condition.

When Adam and Eve ate the prohibited fruit of the tree of the knowledge of good and evil, they realized they were naked. These first two communicating beings then grabbed leaves from a nearby bush and covered themselves. As God approached and called out for them, Adam and Eve hid from Him. God then asked them why they were hiding, and they responded that they were naked. God then asked, "Who *told* you that you were naked?"

Exposed

It seems that the very first consequence of Adam and Eve's decision to eat the prohibited fruit was not that they saw their own nakedness but rather that they saw each other's nakedness. I think the same is true today. We see our nakedness in the eyes of other people, and they sense us peering at them and feel unsettled. But why is that?

God allowed man to eat the fruit of all trees in the garden except one; He prohibited him from the fruit of the tree of the knowledge of good and evil. He didn't do this to tease Adam and Eve or to arouse their curiosity. I don't think it was a power move. God was not—as Satan suggested—fearful that if Adam and Eve ate the forbidden fruit they would become gods just like Him. Yes, Satan had told Eve that if she ate the fruit she would be a god too because she would then know good from evil. And that statement was not entirely false, but not because it might make her a god.

Scripture indicates that Adam was with Eve when she engaged in conversation with the serpent. The discussion led to Eve giving Adam some of the fruit. When they had both eaten the fruit, Scripture says, "The eyes of both were opened, and they knew that they were naked." Their eyes were opened and they knew—they perceived, understood, or became aware of the fact—that they were naked because they saw it in each other's nakedness.

Adam perceived his own nakedness by Eve's expression, by her words, or by her actions. It was the same way for Eve. This is the implication of God's question, "Who told you that you were naked?" Adam's nakedness was just like a milk mustache on someone's upper lip—somebody has to point out it's there.

The youth pastor of a church I attended in the early 1980s was a frequent speaker at youth conferences and youth camps. The day he flew to a youth winter conference in Canada, he contracted some sort of intestinal bug that required him to make frequent trips to the bathroom. As his flight was making the final approach to its destination, he felt the internal summons to sit on the throne for the fourth time in two hours, but the captain had turned on the seat belt sign, so he had to stay in his seat.

When the pastor reached the terminal gate he was focused on finding an airport restroom. But because his flight had arrived late, the group of people meeting him were anxious and behind schedule. The group leader rushed the youth pastor into the first of two waiting cars and put some higher-profile, distinguished guests in the second car of the caravan to the camp. The pastor had no idea that he was in for an hour and a half car ride.

As the car exited the airport and began the climb into the mountains that winter evening, the pastor felt as if he were about to explode. In his mind, he was desperately trying to figure out how to handle the situation. The driver said he knew of no service stations or stores on the way, so the pastor began to watch the second car of the caravan behind him. It was a black, overcast night, and as the front car moved farther ahead of the second car, the pastor hatched a plan. If his timing was just right, he could get the car he was in to pull over, jump into the woods on the side of the road, handle his business, and be back in the car and down the road before the second car caught up. In retrospect, the idea was ridiculous, but at that moment it seemed ingenious.

Finally nature could no longer be restrained, so as the car rounded the top of a curve to the right the pastor yelled at the driver to pull over right then. The startled driver instinctively reacted, and before the car had stopped, the motivated pastor was out and running into the thick brush. In one move his pants were down, and without a second to spare he was crouched on the ground in response to the needs of the virus.

Before he could exhale in relief, the headlights of the car filled with dignitaries rounded the S-curve on the road below and landed squarely on him, lighting him up like a Christmas tree. There he crouched in all his glory.

Rather than having gone into the woods, the pastor had unknowingly merely crossed the small patch of woods that separated the road at the top of the curve from the same road below. The "eyes" of the car—and of all its inhabitants—gazed at his naked body positioned in a rather unflattering way. I don't care how great you think you look naked, the pose of the erupting colon should never be considered if you decide to "strike a pose."

The embarrassed pastor could have explained away his trip into the woods had the plan been successful. However, when the headlights revealed the edge of the road in front of him instead of the safety of the woods, he knew that no explanation would erase the image. As he grabbed at leaves and branches to cover what he could, he knew with certainty that when he arrived at the camp and looked into the eyes of the people in the second car, he would not see them. Instead he would see his own exposed hind end. Maybe that's how Adam and Eve felt.

But hadn't Adam and Eve always been naked? How did they suddenly see nakedness where they hadn't before? Several explanations are possible, but let's look at just two.

Good and Evil

First, the pair may have realized they were naked not because of what they saw but because of how they saw it. When God made the universe, He looked at it and saw it was good. When He made the earth and all its plants and animals, He looked at them and saw that they were good. When God finished creation at the end of the sixth day, Scripture says He looked at it and said it was *very* good. Then God rested. He created, He saw the good in what He created, and then He rested in the good He saw.

I'm sure that He could see the evil, too. Satan appears as a snake in the Garden, tempting Adam and Eve, so it appears that by this time Lucifer had already rebelled and been cast down. Evil could possibly also have existed in some other outpost of the universe. But God certainly wasn't overwhelmed or threatened by the evil, perhaps because He knew that in due course He would deal with it, or it would deal with itself. Evil always destroys itself. Instead, God focused on the good in His creation.

When Adam and Eve chose to disobey, they too could see evil as well as good. Yet they had no idea how to handle it. Without some ability that transcended mere knowledge or absent some kind of tool to manage the knowledge of both good and evil, Adam and Eve were inclined toward the evil. It overwhelmed them.

Remember, they did not eat the fruit of the tree of good and evil. A tree can only produce one kind of fruit—either good or evil. Instead, Adam and Eve ate the fruit of the tree of the *knowledge* of good and evil. They were granted the ability to know—or perceive—both good and evil. But their immediate focus was the evil, and they saw the other person's nakedness as evil.

When Solomon was king of Israel, he recognized that nothing was to be gained from merely knowing both good and evil because man would always lean toward the evil. Instead, Solomon asked for the ability to *discern* good from evil. Things that appeared as good were not necessarily good, and things people quickly judged as evil weren't necessarily evil.

To really live his life and fulfill his duties as king, Solomon needed to be able to discern the good and the evil. He needed the ability to look past the evil and discover the good, and to look past what falsely *appeared* to be good and reject it as evil.

Being naked was not evil. But given the ability to see not just the good in being naked but the bad as well, they erred toward seeing it as evil. Maybe they saw it as tantalizing and with a selfish lust, or as inadequate and offensive—as evidenced by their instant need to cover up. This ability to see good and evil was probably accompanied by words, facial expressions, or actions that exposed the other person's nakedness to that person. Both people perceived the shock of sudden nakedness as evil because they interpreted it as something they must hide. As a result, Adam and Eve did to each other what God would never have done to them: They unwittingly exposed the other person's nakedness in a way that made each of them want to hide.

I wonder if God did not want them to eat from that tree because He wanted them to mature in the good before being exposed to the evil. We do the same thing with our children when we prohibit minors from drinking alcohol. Some foods have an effect that exceeds nutrition, so they must be managed. And the ability to manage is a learned thing. Perhaps God knew Adam and Eve did not have the ability to manage that knowledge, and their disobedience had personal as well as interpersonal consequences.

I suspect that instead of accepting one another, Adam and Eve began evaluating, which prompted that urgent need to cover themselves with leaves. This same sense of self-consciousness reached into all their relationships, including their relationship with God. When they saw God, they still saw only good, but God's image as good made their perception of themselves even more evil.

So the first reason Adam and Eve knew they were naked is that they were unable to manage the knowledge of good and evil. The second reason is somewhat deeper.

Separated

The moment Adam and Eve chose to eat from the tree of knowledge, their internal fire suddenly went out. In an instant, the flame representing their eternal state of being vanished. What do I mean by *fire?*

Scripture says that when God made a covenant with Abraham, He appeared as a smoking firepot and a blazing torch. Later, God appeared to Moses in the form of a burning bush, and He led the Israelites through the wilderness at night by a pillar of fire. When Elijah challenged the prophets of Baal to a contest to identify the true God, he stipulated that the true God would be the one who answered by fire. In the book of Acts, the arrival of the Holy Spirit is signified by tongues of fire extending from heaven down onto the heads of the apostles.

Fire represents eternal existence. When God made us, He breathed His fire into us. That doesn't make us little gods; it makes us children of God. We have His fire as long as we are connected to the source. But sometimes, although the source remains in place, something stands between the source and the flame.

One recent Friday evening my wife and I planned to broil steaks on our gas grill for dinner. I was running late, so I called home and asked my wife to turn on the grill and preheat it. Since she seldom does this, I asked her to take the cordless phone with her out to the patio. I explained how to open the valve on the propane tank and then to turn the gas control knob on the grill to the left so that it pointed to the word *light*. When she finished, I asked her to push the red igniter button several times until she saw the fire in the grill.

She pushed it and pushed it, but nothing happened. We repeated all the steps, but still nothing happened. I was certain she was messing something up, and I thought that if I raised my voice a bit and spoke slowly—as if talking to a deaf person or child—then certainly it would light. Exasperated, I had her turn off the gas and hung up as I drove home, determined to show her how simple this whole procedure really was.

I walked through the front door, put some groceries on the counter, and approached the gas grill like a renowned brain surgeon entering an educational surgery. I walked through the steps I outlined on the phone in an exaggerated fashion, but I had the same result. That was when I discovered the igniter was broken.

God placed a little gas burner in us and connected us to His Spirit. He then gave us a pilot light to ignite our flame and cause it to burn. Our flame— or fire—represents the unique person God made each of us to be. Before the world began, He placed in us the coals and embers of who we would become. As Jesus said, "You are the light of the world," but you have to release or reveal that light if it is to have any impact. That is why you need a pilot light.

The pilot light is the connection between the source—God—and the embers of who God made us to be. The pilot light is always on, and it is always doing the same thing—sparking the desire to know and be known. It is similar to the old-fashioned bellows used in fireplaces. To use bellows, a person repeatedly presses the handles together and then pulls them apart, creating a breeze over the embers and causing them to burst into flame. Like your lungs, the bellows breathe in and out saying, "Know, be known...know, be known...know, be known." That is the pilot light. That is the igniter. God placed it in us.

But at some point in our lives we were enticed by the thought of controlling our own lives...of being our own source of knowledge. When Adam and Eve did this, they turned off the pilot light, effectively causing an impassable gap between the gas and the flame.

"Thanks God, we can take it from here," they seemed to say. "We found a way around Your 'known and be known' system."

The unintended consequence of Adam and Eve choosing their own knowledge was that their flame suddenly went out. They realized they were naked. They looked at each other on the outside and realized something had changed on the inside, which affected the way they looked at the outside. They could tell by the expression on each other's faces that something had changed.

Have you ever heard the axiom, "A disciplined body is the sign of a disciplined mind"?

How about, "You can tell a lot about a person by the way they dress," or "The eyes are the window to the soul"?

Remember Jacob and his limp? The limp was a physical sign of an internal event. Centuries later, Jesus told a crippled man that his sins were forgiven, but He quickly assessed that people would be suspicious of an internal work that could not be validated. So to show that He had the power to forgive sins, He told the man to get up and walk. The physical sign was a window to an internal work. We all commonly use exterior signs to read the interior person.

So, what am I saying? My opinion is that the minute Adam and Eve disobeyed God, their flame went out. They may not have instantly realized what had happened, but they could see something different in each other's eyes. They saw their own nakedness. I think further evidence of this is that they hid from God. Certainly they knew that hiding from God was impossible. Yet, when the flame went out, perhaps they sensed a disconnect. Maybe they suddenly knew that something had changed and that God was somehow external to them. Regardless they were instantly alienated from God, from the people God made them to be, and from each other. They were crouching naked in the bushes in full view of anyone passing by. So they covered themselves and hid.

The Shift

Believe it or not, you probably used to run around the house stark naked and think nothing of it. That's certainly not the case now. Somewhere along the line, your view of nakedness shifted.

When I was living in graduate student housing, many of the students were married with children. A lot of the dorm buildings formed interior courtyards that provided a safe environment for children. Invariably parents would hear a knock at their door, only to answer it and hear that their three-year-old had stripped his clothes off and was running around the courtyard naked. Often the embarrassed parent would run out and scold the clueless child while trying to wrap him like a mummy in the discarded clothes.

At one time each of us ran around the courtyard naked and in plain view of everyone, so to speak. Those of us who are parents probably remember when our children ran through the house naked and never gave it a thought. But one day something changed. Something happened to make our children aware they were naked, and that caused them to start covering up or to close the door when they dressed.

Somewhere back in time, we too became aware of our nakedness and started covering up. We suddenly realized on the *inside* that we were naked on the outside. At the same time, the outside became aware of a fragile, familiar flicker deep inside. Something on the inside was being affected by the actions of the outside. In a very basic, subconscious sense, the outside realized it was a carrier for something unique and personal.

I remember my older sister making me aware of my nakedness when I was four years old. I was lying on my bed in the large bedroom that my sisters and I shared, and I was playing with a toy bow and arrow. It was a late afternoon in August, and I must have been swimming earlier in the day at the community pool in a nearby park because I was naked. I had probably removed the wet swimming suit and started playing, giving little thought to the discarded wet swimming suit on the floor. When I lost the arrow, I started swinging the bow around like a sword. Then, for some unknown reason, I decided to "wear" the bow like a pair of pants.

When my 15-year-old sister walked in I barely noticed her. She is a great sister and very sweet, but I could sense I may have done something wrong as she approached my bed and sat down.

She asked me what I was doing and I said, "Nothing."

She then said, "I promise not to tell if you tell me what you were doing," and sat still, waiting for an answer.

I said nothing because I had no idea what she was talking about or what she was could possibly tell someone. So I just looked at her.

She then said, "Were you playing with yourself?"

In my mind, that was a silly question. She could clearly see there was no one else in the room. Who did she think I was playing with? Did she think I was hiding someone under the bed? Was this a trick? The only thing I could think of was to play along and hope I figured out what she meant. So I looked in her eyes and meekly said, "Yes?"

That seemed to be the right answer because she said okay and got up to leave. But as she did she added the piercing phrase, "But put your shorts on."

Suddenly the person I was playing with—the me on the inside—yelled out to his playmate—the me on the outside—and said, "Hey ... you're naked, you idiot! And because you are, your sister knows I'm in here." I couldn't get dressed fast enough.

I didn't understand what was happening then, but it is clear now that somewhere deep inside I felt uncovered. And though I'm sure I gave little or no thought to the details, I sensed that the gateway to the "me" inside was in some way associated with my nakedness. I never ran around the house unclothed again.

Assumption

At this point I must pause to disclose another assumption. I assume that you have replaced the broker igniter or reignited your pilot light. By that I mean that your flame has no hope of burning unless you intentionally remedy the defect that separates you from your source—from God.

We have each exposed ourselves, sensed the critical stare of others, and acted as if the leaves we quickly grabbed will somehow cover us from their glare. They won't, and you have already discovered that fact. That is why you are certain you will be exposed as you try to make your way through the ditches of life toward home. You can insist on covering yourself with leaves like a man crouching in the woods if you wish, but you have a better option.

After the flame vanished, God still sought out Adam and Eve. They hid from Him just as each of us do, but God pursued them in love to help them be restored.

God will not expose you. Instead, He will cover you—fix the breach between you and Him—and set you back on a course to a place where you were known. It is my hope that this book will introduce the path on which that may happen. But I have to assume that you have taken the steps to reconnect to the source. If not, you should probably put this book down and do so because, if you don't, this book will offer no hope. You will never be able to live before you die. Instead you will die twice, never having lived once.

The Interface

Most people think of nakedness as a physical characteristic. It is. But we also understand that certain body parts are also gateways to the person inside. As a person uncovers and reveals their unique and protected body parts, he opens the door to the inside. The inner and outer persons are directly linked, so we have learned to guard access to the outside because of the potential for rejection and for being misjudged on the inside.

Physical nakedness is inextricably linked to a psychological and spiritual condition. This human outer shell interface functions as a quasi gatekeeper that restricts unauthorized access to our hyper-vulnerable psychological and spiritual inner self. This is where the *being* part of the human resides. The home of the communicating entity.

As we saw in chapter 3, the Bible refers to man as a living being. Man's description—a being—and God's name—I am—are both derived from the verb *be*. Our being is rooted in His name, and our title points to the eternal nature of our existence when it is connected to God.

Your Name

This may seem academic, but it is actually the core of this book. God placed in the human creation an aspect of Himself in the form of an eternal Spirit, which elevated man to a human *being*. But we have each chosen to go our own way, to focus on our self and our own work, to become our own source of knowledge. We want to make a name for ourselves rather than recognizing our association with God's name and trying to rediscover the name He has given us. In a physical sense, you were given a first name by your parents, and your last name—or surname—is your family name. I am Marcus of the Ryans, so to speak.

In a spiritual and eternal sense, you were also given a name that is attached to your Father's name—I Am. God named you just as surely as He named Israel, formerly known as Jacob. Jacob didn't like Jacob, and he wanted to be Esau. But at a poignant moment in his life he unexpectedly wrestled both God and man to discover his true name—Israel. Armed with that name, he was released from trying to *make* a name for himself and went about the business of *being* that name. The time had come for Israel to live.

As the story of Jacob continues past the point where he wrestled himself and God to discover his spiritual name, why isn't Jacob exclusively referred to as Israel? Why is he called Jacob sometimes and Israel others? I'll tell you what I think.

Known by a New Name

Jacob was the physical man known in his birth family and by his neighbors as Jacob. That was the name of his physical body, the shell, the seed. But inside that seed is Israel. Both Jacob and Israel lived for a while, with Jacob growing older and Israel growing up. Jacob was deteriorating, and Israel was maturing. At one point Jacob the body died. Israel didn't. The grave of Jacob contains his body today, but Israel is alive. You too will die. But will you ever live?

My father went by the last name Watkins. Until I was in my twenties, I thought that was his last name. I cannot tell you why, but as I was growing up I never felt attached to that name. For reasons I am only beginning to understand, I wrestled with that name. It just felt foreign to me. I repressed those feelings because I thought my detachment from the name was tantamount to rejecting my father, and that wasn't the issue. I did not struggle with my father. I struggled with the name, and I sensed that somehow my father was also detached from it.

In my twenties I discovered that Watkins was not my father's last name. His father and mother were divorced when he was very young. His mother came from a prominent family in Massachusetts, where her father was a businessman and an attorney, but at the divorce she moved to a very small town in a neighboring state and married a man with the last name Watkins. But before long, my father's mom left her husband and his tiny town and moved to the big city of San Francisco.

My father was given the choice to stay with Mr. Watkins or move with his mother. Because Dad was afraid that his mom would marry again—only to move again—he decided to stay with Mr. Watkins. My father said he wanted a more stable life.

Mr. Watkins was kind to my father, but the extended family often made him feel guilty, telling him he wasn't really a Watkins and that he should be grateful Mr. Watkins let him stay. My dad was the oldest of the six kids in the home. So, with his mother gone, he became responsible to take care of them, to make sure each one had breakfast, and to ensure they arrived at school each day. As the oldest child in the house, he also helped Mr. Watkins in the family business.

Mr. Watkins was the town garbageman, and my father was often embarrassed. He didn't mind the job, but after helping Mr. Watkins on the early morning trash runs, he had to go to school smelling like garbage.

Though I heard many of these stories growing up, I never considered that my dad just *wore* the last name Watkins. None of his legal documents

I was aware of, such as his birth certificate or military discharge papers, used that name. He was never adopted. I never once heard my father refer to Mr. Watkins as his father or as Dad, yet I was totally surprised the day he walked into my office in Laguna Hills, California, and said he was considering going back to his real last name.

My dad was in his sixties at that point, so the idea of casting off a name he was known by most of his life was not a small thing. But when he revealed that our family name was not Watkins, I felt as if a light turned on inside of me. I wasn't really a Watkins either. My feelings had nothing to do with the name. Watkins is a fine name, and my younger brother still goes by that name, but even he recognized my struggle and lack of attachment to the name.

Somehow, my father's lifelong internal struggle (which was only revealed late in his life) had been my struggle as the eldest son all my life. I knew that the name I had worn to that point in my life didn't reflect who I really was on the inside, and my father's willingness to reveal his struggle—even that late in life—brought the reality of the battle to the surface. I no longer had to ignore the conflict or flagellate myself for the thoughts and feelings I had. I finally knew why I felt like a frog in a snake.

Have you ever seen a snake that has eaten a frog? You can see the frog moving down the length of the snake, inching from the mouth toward the tail until it is finally digested and gone. That's how I felt. The real me seemed to be moving down the throat of a snake of a man, and if I didn't respond to that fact soon I would be digested and *unable* to react.

My dad ultimately dismissed the idea of recovering his family name because he didn't want to confuse all his friends and acquaintances in the small town where he lived. They would have probably thought he was senile. But although it may have been too late for my dad to throw off that old name, I had no such restraints in my mind. So with my father's blessing, I made a phone call to an attorney to reclaim my name.

Sure, when I go back to my hometown some folks are confused. Some people still refer to me by my old name, and that's fine. That is how they knew me. But my identity is reattached to a new name.

In the same way, Jacob would still be Jacob to some people. But my personal opinion is that the Jacob on the outside recognized the spiritual man on the inside named Israel. And Jacob's duty was to help Israel live in a way that released Israel when Jacob the seed died and was buried in the ground. Our bodies will either work against us or work for us.

Seed

Human beings may be the only creatures who bury their dead. Abundant evidence indicates that primitive man took the time to cover the body and bones of those who died rather than leaving them in the open—exposed. They also carried those bodies back to their camps or homes rather than burying them in an unknown place. Civilizations have always had a certain amount of respect for dead bodies.

The Sunday evening my father died, his bedroom was filled with friends, children, grandchildren, and great-grandchildren. When men from the mortuary arrived, they waited in the hallway for us to finish a time of prayer and reflection around my father's body. After a few minutes everyone left the room except my younger brother and me, which cleared the way for the mortuary workers and their gurney. They then stepped back and asked if my brother and I would like to lift my father's dead body onto the gurney and into the body bag. After we had done so, I zipped the body bag up and over his face, and together my brother and I walked alongside my father's body as the mortuary workers wheeled it out to their vehicle. I stood at the end of the driveway for some time after they drove away, realizing that I would never see him in this life again.

But his body had done its job well. His family and friends knew him, and he knew each of us uniquely, because he took the time to seek us out, to reveal himself, and to give selflessly. But he didn't do that with just anyone and everyone. He knew that a person must walk the fine line between revealing and concealing.

My dad knew that sometimes we just need a place where we can hear what we think. Places in which we can safely speak our thoughts and examine them. But physical nakedness taught us to cover the private areas and reserve them for the proper setting and person. We don't strip naked and walk around in plain view of everyone and subject ourselves to the scrutiny of strangers. Likewise, our bodies learned to protect our spirits so that we don't recklessly or abruptly open up personal thoughts and feelings to just anyone. On one hand, we must not expose who we are to anyone and everyone, and the other, we dare not protect who we are to such a degree that we prohibit even ourselves from accessing that person.

The Body

My father's body was planted like a seed, and it released a mature spirit that was known by God. God knew my father's true name. I think that is why he was willing to reexamine the name he wore so late in life. Why would someone who guarded that internal anguish his whole life do that? Because his spirit had matured and was ready to be released. You see, just a few short years after that day in my office, my father heard God call his true name. The seed of Arthur Watkins would die and bear fruit. It would release the fire.

Your body is somewhat oblivious to the fact that it will die and is in fact already dying. Your spirit—your fire—keeps reminding your body of this fact, but your body tends to dismiss its desperate cries, as if it seems to think that death will happen to others, but not you. Your physical or carnal nature desires to serve itself and seek its own way. Its instinct is to dominate everything, including the person you really want to be.

But your body isn't bad; it's just simple. It is animallike—satisfying its appetites, testing its power, and chasing its tail for entertainment. We are easily entertained, aren't we? We just need to go faster or be extreme about something. Being who God made us to be seems pointless. It sounds like a confusing exercise in futility. We prefer fun or a physical challenge.

Yet your body is the capsule of life and holds your true fire. It is a seed. Remember, a seed does not die and produce a seed. It dies and produces a tree, for instance. The life that comes out of the seed is not the same thing as the seed. The body doesn't die to produce another body. It dies to release the fire. Its purpose is to protect the fire until it is ready to be released, and it awaits the day the two will be reunited in a new, almost unimaginable way.

Let's Rumble

When I was in junior high my Sunday school teacher took my class on a weekend campout at a lake near Ashland, Oregon. One late afternoon just before dinner, I walked down to the lakeshore by myself. As I strolled next to the water, I was shocked to see a fairly large snake just a little way ahead of me, just barely out of the water.

The snake wasn't moving, so I thought it might be dead. But as I cautiously approached I realized it had nearly swallowed a large frog. All that remained outside the snake was the last inch or so of its hind end, but its shape was clearly visible in the snake's mouth and neck.

I had never seen a snake eat a frog before. For a while I stood and watched with a combination of curiosity and revulsion. I realized that what was happening was a natural part of life, and what the snake was now doing to the frog, the frog had probably just done to some other creature. But for some reason it seemed wrong to me. I don't know why, but something came over me, and I had to intervene.

I found a large stick and started beating the snake with a ferocity that bordered on vengeance. I was determined to get that frog out of the snake. I beat that snake from head to tail over and over again, and for quite a while nothing happened. I began to think that I was too late to save the frog and that all I was going to do was kill the poor snake.

But slowly the snake began to spit the frog out. I continued to beat the snake, and eventually it began to release the frog a fraction of an inch at a time. I probably beat that snake on and off for 20 minutes before the frog was fully expelled.

Exhausted and a little shaken, I sat down on a log. I watched the snake slowly move toward the lake, and after 15 minutes or so it was half in and half out of the water.

For a long time the frog showed no signs of life other than an occasional blink of its eye. Finally I saw it move one back leg...just a little. About that time my teacher called us in for dinner, and I left to eat. When I came back about half an hour later the frog was moving around pretty well, showing few physical signs of the encounter other than the snake spit on its back. The snake, however, was dead.

I think it is time that we, as men, begin to fight. We need to pick up a stick and start beating the frog out of ourselves. Your body will serve itself, or it will serve the eternal being God made you to be. What you choose to do determines if you will have a chance to ever really live. You just need to know that either way, your body dies.

Moving the Fire

In 1877, the United States government required the Ponca Indians living in the Southeast United States to move to Oklahoma. The operation was an attempt to resolve land disputes, and it became known as the Trail of Tears. The move was very difficult for the tribe, and the foul weather and disease made it even more so. About one-third of the Poncas making the journey died within two years of reaching Oklahoma.

These Native Americans could take very few belongings with them, which meant that most of what they owned was left behind. But they would *not* leave behind their sacred fires. Bundles of ash and cinders from these sacred fires were carried the vast distance, each being nurtured and replenished as the journey continued.

Primitive man also had to move his fire from place to place and guard it with ferocity. Absent the knowledge to create fire, ancient man had to capture it. He had to watch for lightning strikes or forest fires, seize the fire from one of these sources, and thereafter guard it aggressively. Without fire, he had no warmth and no protection from wild beasts. He had to eat his food raw. Any person who has had to survive the wilderness will tell you fire is one of man's most important possessions.

The same is true for our identity. We must guard it with an intensity that borders on viciousness. The fire of our identity originated in God and in the work of His Son, and the coals that burn bright red are the traits and tendencies that our parents and certain others in our youth recognized and fanned. Our fire was kindled and nurtured in our home and in our sphere of life.

But is this true for you? Perhaps your home was not a nurturing place, and your sphere of life was harsh. No one kindled your fire. Instead, they poked and prodded it, and all you heard was others lamenting that you wouldn't burn the way they wanted you to. They were trying to use your flame to warm themselves before it had even really ignited.

So you had to watch for a source of ignition. Perhaps a lightning strike out of the blue, such as a relationship with someone outside your home. Maybe it was personal success in an area of interest that sparked a flame from which you captured your fire. It has probably been hard to maintain, but even though it may not be a roaring bonfire, it is still burning.

By now you have probably discovered that every man must eventually move his fire. You must leave the home of your youth, the area that gave you a sense of *place,* and continue your journey. You must return to the fire of origin, to the source, to the place you were forged. Your fire can never mature unless you continue your quest to be known.

But moving the fire is not an easy thing to do. During this time you are particularly vulnerable, and you have no guarantee that the fire will survive. Knowing the destination in advance would make the move easier for you because then you would chart a path and prepare the way. But like the Poncas who were forced on a trek to find a place known only by its name— Oklahoma—you know only that you must make the journey.

Some men will never reach the end of the next, crucial phase with their fire still viable. All sorts of other things will try to make its way into the fire. Some of it will be fuel that is useful, such as friends and accomplishments. Some of it will be debris and unburnable waste that either bogs the fire down or ignites an uncontrollable wildfire. Jobs or material possessions can have this effect. Some things may even try to extinguish or retard the fire because of misunderstanding or jealousy. For those reasons you must guard and care for your fire as you journey toward the goal. The Poncas had to find Oklahoma. As we will see in the next chapter, you must find a hearth.

8

THE HEARTH

THE FIRST MORNING I entered my third-floor office in northeast Atlanta, I had a visitor. A small cardinal landed on the brick window ledge and began to tap on the glass in what I interpreted as a sign of welcome. No one had occupied that particular office for a little while, so I suspected the bird was happy to have some company. After tapping for a few minutes he flew away, only to return again and resume his tireless pecking.

What had been endearing the first morning quickly became very irritating. Every day, perhaps a dozen times a day, the bird landed on the ledge and spent about half an hour pecking on the glass before flying away. By my fourth day in that office I was at my wit's end with the bird. The next time he landed on the ledge I took a newspaper and smacked the glass at the exact point and time the bird pecked it. The bird jumped and flew back about 18 inches, but rather than scaring him away, the loud *bang* against the glass merely excited him. He had feedback! He landed on the ledge and resumed his pecking with renewed intensity.

I wondered why the bird was incessantly trying to get in and why he had no fear of me whatsoever. Then I realized that he wasn't trying to get in at all. That bird never saw me. The windows in my office were coated with a film that reflected the light and heat, so each time the bird came to my window, it acted like a mirror for him. In his mind he came to visit his little friend.

Sometimes I felt like yelling in Al Pacino fashion, "Oh yeah? Say hello to *my* little friend," while squeezing the trigger of an air horn. I've gotten so frustrated with that bird that I've been tempted to climb onto the roof with a broom, lean over the edge, and play badminton with a real birdie.

Sometimes the bird would just peck. Other times he would leap up against the glass and batter it with his wings, often jumping in successive attacks up the full height of the window. I thought I'd seen it all, but one day I watched the bird land on the ledge with a worm in his mouth. He spent about five minutes trying to feed that worm to his own reflection in the glass.

The bird might have felt as if his day was filled with friends, battles, and caring for others. But the fact of the matter is, regardless of what the bird perceived, no one was in that window but himself. His complete and sole attention was directed at himself. He interacted with no one. He battled no one. He fed no one.

That entire summer I watched a bird that was convinced he was involved with the world around him, when in fact the bird himself was the only one in his world. I thought of G.K. Chesterton's comment: "How much bigger your world would be if you were just smaller in it."

All by Myself

Motivated by a force deep within that stirs while we are yet in our youth, we men reach a point at which we set out to make our own way. The once-distant echo of the call of the wild grows closer, and it beckons each of us to follow. And we are compelled to respond. We must establish our own den and find our place in the pack.

The call is at once exciting and forbidding, and we set off hopeful that we can rise above the fray and that we will carve out a unique place in the world around us. We set and meet goals. We engage in challenges with mixed results. The task of finding the right woman is but one of many conquests. All the while we swing the bag filled with the embers and ashes of our fire from shoulder to shoulder, at times even forgetting they are there.

We can easily spend substantial time and energy doing things we perceive as meaningful. We spend our early years in the journey going from one place to another, overcoming obstacles, and battling the competition. Occasionally we feel the internal satisfaction of helping others. We may even get married, have a family, and provide a nice home. But more often than not we are simply pecking on the window of life.

We go to bed at night remembering the events of the day, oblivious to the fact that—like the bird—the only person we really engaged was ourself. If we stopped to think, we would realize that we know little about the people with whom we thought we were interacting. We made assumptions based on the way they responded to us, but we never saw them *apart* from us. We see the body, but we know nothing of the person inside.

Even if the bird had realized all he was seeing was his own image, what would he have learned about himself? Wouldn't he merely have reinforced his own perception? Sure, he may have bolstered his self-esteem, but he did nothing for his *true* esteem.

I've known men like that, and I'm sure at times I too have been like that. We all have. I know a man who is now in his mid-forties and who has spent the better part of his life watching himself in the window of life. He is enormously talented, wealthy, and well-known, but he seems to be spending his life admiring the man in the mirror. On a stroll through a shopping center several years ago, he spent the majority of his time trying to decide if he should buy six or seven pairs of the exact same expensive tennis shoe. I don't think he will ever marry because he would have to divorce himself to do so.

But eventually most of us realize that the road we have taken to become the man we want to be is not turning out the way we thought it would. The excitement of being young, virile, and strong has weaned. We begin to suspect that what we thought would be a sprint to glory has become a marathon with no end in sight and no guarantee that we will find what we seek.

The Image

In July of 1982, I was riding through South Dakota on a tour bus with a group of young musicians. Several people were asleep that sunny morning when the bus driver yelled out that we were approaching an exit to Mount

Rushmore. When we had charted that day's course the night before, none of us realized we would be so close to this magnificent monument featuring the faces of four former United States presidents chiseled into the rock. Most of us knew we would not be this close to Mount Rushmore again.

The driver said the site was just a little over 40 miles away, and he thought we could be there in less than an hour. We made a spontaneous decision to seize the opportunity just in time for him to steer the bus toward the exit and head up the mountain.

At first the excursion seemed great, and we opened some of the windows to catch the fresh mountain air. But very soon the bus slowed considerably as it reached the steep pitch in the highway and began to maneuver the hairpin turns that led to the top of the mountain. The bus swayed back and forth as it navigated the sharp, narrow road. Everyone began to feel sick, and our initial excitement to see the monument faded because of our incredibly slow progress up the steep mountain road. More than two hours after we exited the freeway, the bus pulled into the parking lot of the visitors' center.

As we slowly began to exit we realized that a weather front had moved in, and a cloud had settled on the face of the mountain. Still, we entered the visitors' center, paid the requisite fee, and walked out onto the large cement viewing platform with anticipation.

Our excitement once again dimmed as we looked up at where the massive faces were chiseled into the rock and saw only clouds. None of the monument was visible—we couldn't see one president. We strolled back and forth across the long viewing area, hoping to get an angle to peer through the clouds, but to no avail. Not only had the trip been nearly three times as long as we anticipated, but now we realized that we had driven that distance only to stare into clouds. We could have driven through a fog bank and had the same experience. Reluctantly we got back on the bus and drove away.

The Mirror

Like the bird at my office, some of us are content to simply interact with ourselves, seemingly oblivious to the fact that we never get more than a superficial understanding of who we might be. Some live their lives *doing*. For others, the pressure of *doing* gives way to the satisfaction of *being*. Yet for that to happen, we need to really see ourselves and somehow access the person inside—the person we were made to be.

That might sound easy. But perhaps like me on my journey to the monument, you have discovered that catching a glimpse of the great person you were made to be is not so simple. It has taken much more time than you anticipated, and as much as you strain your eyes to see the person you truly want to be, the image etched into the mountain eludes you. It is hidden in the fog of life.

The more you stare, the more despondent you become. You sense you must recover the person you think God made you to be, yet you are separated from that image by the person you've become. The more we see of who we are, the harder we struggle to see the person we really *want* to be. We need a mirror that lets us see the inside—see the character and nature of the person others see. But how? What kind of mirror could possibly do that?

Let me tell you right up front where I am going with this. I am convinced that one of the best mirrors available to help you access the person you were made to be is your wife. I realize you may not be married, you may no longer be married, or you may already be married. Each of those conditions is replete with its own advantages and challenges. But before we examine your unique case, let's take a step back and look at the general model of marriage.

Ideally, your wife both projects and reflects your image and provides you a safe place of self-discovery. Unlike your parents, your wife had no obligation to associate herself with you or love you. She chose to do so, and you chose to love her, which creates the potential for mutual self-discovery. Marriage challenges us to move past our own interests and engage someone else's. Marriage becomes a mutual and gradual peeling back of the layers, a process of physical, emotional, and spiritual nakedness lasting a lifetime.

But even as I say this, you may reject that idea either experientially or philosophically. You may be married, or you have been married, and your wife didn't see the real you or the person God made you to be. Instead she saw either the person you weren't or the person *she* wanted you to be.

In some cases the marriage mirror has become more like a carnival mirror—distorting the reflection. Because a carnival mirror is bent in its design, it can cause the average person to appear very tall and skinny or short and fat. It intentionally gives you a warped image of yourself.

A carnival mirror provides great entertainment for kids, but you don't want to use one to pick out which clothes to buy, to shave your face, or to get dressed in the morning. And you don't want to marry a woman who is warped in the way she sees you, sees others, or sees herself. Some men exercise such contol over their wives that they unintentionally *cause* them to reflect a warped image, thereby nullifying a significant benefit of the marriage relationship.

Perhaps you are single and have no intention of ever marrying. Given the difficulty most marriages face, I can certainly understand a person taking that position. But a time comes when most of us recognize that we are on a long wilderness journey, and we simply need to find someone with whom we can establish a unique, long-term relationship. We must find that certain person who holds the key to us and for whom we do the same. We must find a place to set the ashes and embers we began carrying when we first set out to move our fire.

When God first presented the woman to Adam, Adam was ecstatic. He recognized that the woman had the potential to understand and help him in a way no other creature could because she was made from his own bones—from the same mold. Adam also recognized that the woman was taken out of him. In a broad sense, he looked at the woman and saw himself. Eve could help Adam see himself in a detached sort of way, as if he were holding himself up at arm's length and examining who he was. The woman was like a mirror.

For a period of time in the Garden of Eden, woman was just that—woman. As you read the account of the disobedience and the fall of man in the garden, Adam is referred to as Adam but the woman has no name. She is simply *the woman*. She was a category.

But after they saw each other's nakedness and received their punishment, Adam *named* Eve. She was no longer a mere category—a woman. She was a specific person—she was Eve. Facing banishment and a long journey through the wilderness, Adam needed a certain person.

Yada Yada

Once Adam named Eve, the Scripture says he *knew* her, and she conceived. Freud argued that man's libido—his desire for sex—drives his whole life. He believed sexual desires and the conflicting attitudes associated with them were at the core of man's thoughts and behavior. Freud recognized an attribute in man, but he mischaracterized it. He believed sexual drive to be the core issue of man, when libido is actually a means of addressing the core issue. This is clear in this Hebrew text of Genesis.

The word translated *knew* is the Hebrew word *yada*. Think of the phrase "yada yada," which essentially means, "you know, you know." But this word is not merely a conversational shortcut, the verbal equivalent of fast-forwarding through a section the speaker assumes the listener already understands. The Bible does not always use this word to reference sexual relationships, which indicates that its use here is intentional.

An airline recently featured an in-flight movie about two couples. The plot detailed the interactions within each couple as well as those between the couples. As the movie progressed, each man became interested in the other man's wife. I was working on my laptop and only vaguely listening, but my interest was stirred when I realized that one of the men found out his wife had an affair with the other man.

The betrayed husband immediately wanted to know the details. "Where did you have sex?" "Was he any good?" "Did you like it?" "Was he better than me?"

If nakedness and sex are about pursuit and conquest, or are simply a means to personal satisfaction, then who cares what the wife thinks? Why should a man care that another man paid homage as long as the affair didn't conflict with his personal schedule or cost him any money?

A sexual relationship is one means to know someone and be known by them. The core of a man's thoughts and behavior is not libido, but the desire to know and be known. When a husband and wife engage in sexual relations in a context that facilitates the process of knowing and being known, the result is conception. It produces life.

You know your wife physically, and she conceives a baby. You know your wife emotionally and spiritually—and are known by her emotionally and spiritually—and she consistently conceives new life in your fire. She blows on your embers. She becomes the hearth for your fire.

Your wife is the place in your home that holds the flame of the person God made you to be, and incredibly, she provides a way for you to sit by that fire in the fireplace and see the flame. In a profound and almost mystical way you can actually see with your own eyes that seemingly elusive person God made you to be. As the apostle Paul said, "He who loves his wife loves himself." No wonder marriage is a profound mystery.

A wife doesn't make you that person. A wife draws that person out of you and helps *you* see him. Then, just as Eve helped Adam, your wife helps you do what God called you to do. She knows you, she then reveals that person to you, you then see that person, and you have the opportunity to rise to the challenge of becoming that person. What a gift!

The Hearth

When I was in the sixth grade, a friend and I started building a tree house in the field behind my house. Partway through the first day, a couple of older guys in the neighborhood joined in, and with their help we built a massive fort in the small apple tree. By the middle of the third day of construction my friend and I were finalizing the inside by tacking down some old carpet someone had thrown out. The three older guys were on the ground outside, trying to find one more old 2x4 to finish the ladder rungs we nailed to the tree.

My friend and I laid the carpet and had just finished installing the lock on the inside when we decided to lock the older guys out. We secured the door and then taunted them by saying we weren't going to let anyone in. Big mistake.

The oldest guy outside said, "You better open that door now and let us in, or we'll burn you out of there."

We looked at each other as if to say, "Sure...right, I bet you will," and we continued to laugh. We laughed and laughed...until the smoke filled the tree house, at which time we stopped laughing, unlocked the door, and jumped out, all in one move.

The guys outside glanced at us as we hit the ground, and then they turned their heads back toward the tree house. The bottom of the tree house was engulfed in flames, and the dry grass around the base had caught fire. That fire was spreading out from the area around the tree to the dry alfalfa in the field. In minutes the fire department arrived to keep the fire from spreading past the field and into a housing development, but it was too late for the tree house. No one ever played in it. We spent three days building it, my friend and I spent about five minutes locked inside laughing at how clever we were, and then it was gone.

Fire is not a toy. In its native state it is a powerful force that exists in only one of two extremes: A fire either burns out of control or it burns out. Left alone, it is either one or the other; there is no in between or constant state. That is why man had to learn to harness and manage the dangerous and delicate properties of fire.

The flame called *you* is a powerful force. Left to itself it is unfocused and unruly. Yet it is also vulnerable. For those reasons you need a hearth. You must have someplace where you can release, manage, and protect the fire. That hearth is a wife.

A hearth gives the fire a sense of place. It provides a boundary for the fire while ensuring that it continues to burn. Ashes and embers from the past form a sort of insulation beneath the fire, and the fire becomes rich, warm, and inviting. One of the best things a wife does is take you off the road. She gives you a place to be.

In 1980 I worked as a trainer for a company based in Chicago. The job required me to stay in hotels an average of 26 days a month. I thought it was a very cool way to live...for a while. But after the first six months of never unpacking my suitcase, it became a little less cool. Sure, when I told people about the job, they usually thought it was a great way to live, and I didn't let on that it wasn't as cool as it sounded. Yet I began to seek a promotion simply as a way to get off the road.

This place is a hearth, which is your wife. And in addition to a sense of place, it also provides protection. By that I mean, after a day struggling through the battles of work and life, you need to be able to sit in the big overstuffed chair by the hearth, look at the flame, and be reminded of who you really are. Throughout the day you encounter all sorts of people who challenge or chip away at that person. People who know nothing about you question the person you are trying to become. When you return to the hearth, you are reminded that those people know nothing of the true you. That person has been protected by the hearth.

Years ago, two close friends of mine and I worked together for a time with a brilliant but rather unscrupulous man. We didn't know he was unscrupulous at the time; instead, we thought he was the key to our future. The more we worked in this environment, the more we tried to become the people this man needed us to be. We thought he really saw our potential and that he desired to mold us into great—and wealthy—young businessmen.

Years later, after painfully extricating ourselves from the web we helped weave, we discovered that fairly early on in the process our wives independently reached a different conclusion. I knew that my wife didn't trust that man, and she told me several times that she felt he was trying to use our reputation and connections to bolster his, not the other way around. This seemed ludicrous to me, but the more I heard this from her, the more I saw the truth behind what I had been seeing. My wife was right.

As I talked candidly with my two friends, they disclosed that their wives were saying the same thing. This wasn't a conspiracy between wives because my wife didn't have the chance to spend much time with their wives. Instead, each of our wives knew us better than we knew ourselves. They kept the flame safe, and their commitment to reveal that fire to us each night as we sat by the hearth finally led us to take abrupt action we may not have taken if left to ourselves.

Ashes and Embers

Our wives serve in many other ways as the hearth for the flame of the people God made us to be, but I want to finish with one final characteristic of the hearth. Your wife holds your ashes.

As your flame burns throughout your life, it creates the ashes of who you were…the memories of life. Those ashes are a significant part of your life story. The longer your flame burns in the hearth of your wife, the richer and more dense the ashes become. When you die your wife continues to display your ashes and tell your story. But divorce sweeps the hearth clean. It separates you from your memories. The person who recollects with you is gone, and you can't turn to her and say, "Remember when we…"

Years ago I purchased one of those small, low-resolution cameras and mounted it on my computer monitor. One day when my kids were nine, seven, and four, they came into my home office. When I showed them how the camera took video clips, they spontaneously launched into a hillbilly version of "Jesus Loves the Little Children." I loved that clip and played it quite often. A few years later I had other computers and laptops, and I only used the computer with that clip occasionally. One day as I booted up the computer I got the "blue screen of death." I couldn't recover that video file on that computer, and when I went to replace it from the backup CD I discovered that the CD was corrupted as well. The video linked me to rich memories and helped me relive a cherished moment. But it was gone.

Who will hold your ashes and tell your story? I realize that some men have no hearth, but I believe that sometimes certain men still seek one out.

A woman I know received a notice from the registrar of wills in a far-off state. She was surprised to discover that a man she didn't really know had left her a small dispersement at his death. When she later received a copy of the final accounting she realized that the man had absolutely no one in his life. At his death the executor of the estate even had to pay someone to clean out his apartment and throw away what little personal possessions the man owned. No one cared for him at death, and no other person was named in the will. He left the woman a very modest sum of money and two screenplays he had written. He left nothing else…it was all thrown away.

As I talked with this woman about the man, we began to ponder the events leading up to his death. We knew the man was a Christian, and we sensed he knew when he created the will that death was not too far off. Absent a family or friend to remember him or his work when he died, could he have really prayed about what to do with the token of possessions he had accumulated? Perhaps the God who made this man and who knew his heart somehow said, *I'll tell you what to do. I know a woman who will guard the ashes of your memory. When you die, you give your "ashes" to this woman.*

The man had few material goods and clearly knew no one. But he had two screenplays. As much as the screenplays tell a factional story, they also tell a story of the man who wrote them. The stories he wrote and the characters developed were culled from his own life, and in a unique way they told his story. He knew little of the woman he left these things to, and she knew little of him. But God knew them both, and God knew that this man—even if only at the time of his death—needed a hearth.

Betrayed

To bring home the point that marriage is a relationship centered in knowing and being known, let me tell you about a small study I conducted.

I was curious to know if men and women who were victims of infidelity processed the betrayal differently. If we consider both the rational thoughts and the emotional experience associated with adultery, do men and women feel the *sting* uniquely?

I'm sure you've heard phrases like "He knew her...in a biblical sense." So I put together a ten-question survey that used the term *know* to represent sexual relations. Five questions were worded uniquely to ask, "If your spouse admitted infidelity, would the feeling of betrayal be centered around the concept that *someone else knew* your spouse," and another five questions focused on the concept that *your spouse knew* someone else. It may seem to be the same thing, but the results showed a clear distinction between the way men and women experienced it. Remember, it wasn't an either/or question as much as one concerning which feeling was stronger.

Men were significantly more concerned that another man knew his wife, while the woman felt empty because her husband knew another woman. Does that seem to be the same thing? Let me explain the difference using the image of the hearth.

Men were furious that another man entered his house and used his hearth. Men know that a wife holds some unique part of them, and they have no intention of sharing that private, personal world. But suddenly the hearth contains another man's ashes as well as his own, and each night as he comes home and sits by the hearth and gazes into the fire of *The Man God Made Him to Be,* he sees bits of the other man's ashes. A hearth cannot contain two fires. When it does, it has become an ashtray.

The woman, on the other hand, felt the fire move. She was no longer *the place;* she was *a place.* No longer unique. She was migrating back from a name—Eve—to a category—woman—and she could sense the change. She knew that before long, the ashes and embers would be abandoned, the hearth would be swept clean, and the fire would try to start over somewhere else. How many times does a woman help a man both see and become the person

God made him to be, only to be left behind when the man senses he has become that person?

When I moved from California to Virginia to enter graduate school, my wife was eight months pregnant with our third child. We lived in graduate student housing for four years in an apartment my wife called a storage facility with a kitchenette. Just two months after giving birth, she started a full-time job so I could go to school. Though I began to work again the following year, my wife carried the load through my master's program and my doctorate.

Can you imagine how my wife would have felt if, as I walked off the graduation platform after receiving my Ph.D., I strolled up to her and said, "I'm Dr. Ryan now. I did it all myself. I need to find someone who fits this new image."

I'm sure that while I was waiting for the paramedics to arrive I would have heard her say, "You are only Dr. Ryan because I helped you see that person. You didn't do it yourself. *We* did it."

The Ideal

As I write this chapter, I fully understand that your wife may not be a hearth for you. She may have let you down in many ways and may even admit doing so.

You and your wife could discuss all the reasons your marriage isn't working out the way you each thought it would, but in the process you would probably begin to polarize. Though your viewpoints are undoubtedly valid, and your expectations and hurt are very real, polarization is not going to help you live before you die.

Following the path to being known will help you avoid the path to polarization. The path to being known is always a difficult path, and it is littered with discarded masks and expectations. In contrast, the path to polarization is the easier path at first, but along that path lie the dead bones of millions of viable marriages, each one buried beneath a library of reasons.

I don't know all the circumstances surrounding your marriage, so I would be both presumptive and careless to give you a list of five things you can do to remake your marriage. But I can tell you this. Regardless of how bad it is, what you have or haven't done, or what your wife has or hasn't done, your relationship can be fixed. It won't be easy, but the code of "know and be known" can give you the understanding you need to begin, and the time and energy you put into it can yield tremendous results.

The $1.5 billion Hubble Space Telescope was launched amid tremendous excitement and hope. Mankind would finally get a glimpse of the stars and planets they knew were out there, but had been inaccessible. As scientists attempted to use the telescope to peer deep within the universe in hopes of discovering its secrets, they quickly realized that something was wrong. One of Hubble's lenses had not been properly ground, which made the images fuzzy and unclear. Therefore, the pictures sent back to earth were no better than those scientists had been taking from earth. The Hubble telescope gave man no better images than he had before the launch.

So scientists spent a tremendous amount of time and the United States government spent tens of millions of dollars developing a plan to correct the lens. They had no guarantee of success, but walking away from it wasn't an option. Ultimately, the plan worked, and the result was a space telescope that produced images beyond imagination. We now see stars being formed in distant galaxies we had no hope of seeing apart from the rescue mission.

Your marriage may not have given you the images of yourself you hoped it would on the day you said "I do," but that doesn't mean it cannot do so. It just means it hasn't done so because of an undetected fundamental error. The lenses just need to be corrected. I am convinced God knows the way, and He desires to walk you and your wife through it.

9

THE THING

Let the favor of the Lord our God be upon us,
and establish the work of our hands upon us;
yes, establish the work of our hands!
PSALM 90:17

....

JUSTO GALLEGO MARTINEZ entered a monastery as a young man, and he fully intended to spend the rest of his life as a monk serving God and the church. But when he contracted tuberculosis, the abbot feared Justo would trigger an outbreak throughout the monastery, so he expelled him. The reversal dropped Justo into a time of deep depression.

Most of us would interpret the ejection from the monastery as a release from our vocation, and we would spend the rest of our life either resenting God or trying to find another purpose. But Justo still believed his vocation was to be a monk. He was supposed to build the church. The only thing he needed to determine was how God wanted him to pursue it. His depression began to lift.

Justo isn't sure exactly what prompted his actions one day in 1961, but in the fall of that year the 36-year-old monk sold some land he had inherited and began to build a cathedral. He started by digging out an area in the ground that would later become a crypt under the main floor, and thereafter he began to erect the exterior walls.

For the past 45 years Justo has worked ten hours a day, every day of every week, every week of every year. He has no crane or machinery, but rather works with some rickety old scaffolding rising 100 feet into the air, and an occasional volunteer. He received no funding from the Catholic church or the Spanish town of Mejorada del Campo, yet he found ways to secure the material he needed at the moment he needed it.

Today the cathedral measures 86,000 square feet and features a cross that rises 121 feet into the air. It is a beautiful structure with cloisters, minor chapels, and a library. Each day the 80-year-old Justo prays to God and asks for the five additional years of life he believes he needs to finish the work.

Only recently has anyone outside that small town in Spain paid any attention to the cathedral, and only because Justo and the cathedral were featured in a TV commercial for bottled water. Even now, neither the town nor the Catholic church provides any support—monetary or otherwise.

Undaunted and unfazed, Justo continues to work, saying he is a monk by vocation and a laborer by destiny. His life has been filled with challenges and rejection. He faced a potentially debilitating disease and a serious crisis of purpose in midlife. Yet, at 80 years old, Justo is secure in his work. He truly believes he is supposed to do just one thing—build a cathedral.

Work

What are you supposed to do? Do you continue to return to one thing regardless of the disappointments and setbacks? When or where do you feel God's pleasure?

I've heard countless sermons, lectures, and motivational speeches telling men that they are not what they do. We are told to stop defining ourselves by our jobs or careers. But I don't think man can separate his identity from his vocation because I can't see where God separated it, or relegated his work to an appendage of his life. When God speaks of man in the early chapters of Genesis it is often in the context of his effect on the earth. His work. Also, the apostle Paul wrote that a man who is not willing to work should not be fed.

All living things—vegetation, animals, and man—are instructed to multiply and fill the earth. But in addition to that command, man is instructed to take dominion and subdue the earth. The context of the edict makes clear that man is supposed to be God's general manager—His physical representative on the earth. Man is infused with both the ability and the authority to bring order out of chaos and to assist created matter in finding its fullest expression. We are to be God's hands that till the soil and work the ground, creating an environment in which all that God has already created finds its individual and intended expression. We are to continue what God started. We are to do the work of our Father.

We see this exhibited in the life of Jesus when He commented that, as God's Son, He was to be about the Father's business. The picture is of an active household doing the work of an involved Father. Jesus said, "Whatever the Father does, that the Son does likewise." If Jesus was consistently restoring spiritual, emotional, and physical health to mankind, and if He calmed the waves and called on a fig tree to produce fruit or wither and die, then that is exactly what He saw His Father doing.

Do you know what God made you to do in the family business? We each have an intrinsic desire to put our hand to *something,* yet many of us mistakenly believe that our vocation is somehow detached from our spiritual life. So most of us really never engage in God's work. Instead, we go to church and read the Bible. Then we either punch the clock in futility or set sail on the sea of life. We determine to go our own way and find our own purpose.

But *we have no purpose* outside of that which God placed in us. Apart from His purpose, we have only meaningless activity that keeps us busy. Will a merely busy life provide satisfaction while we live or at the point of death?

God's punishment in the Garden of Eden didn't change Adam's purpose— or ours. God provided no alternative—no "plan B." Adam was still required to expand throughout the earth and bring order, and also to stimulate creation to find *its* unique expression. But just as disease made Justo's calling more difficult, the disease of sin associated with Adam's rebellion made both his and Eve's tasks harder. Pain was now associated with multiplying and being fruitful, and toil and sweat would accompany Adam's work. But God did not remove or change His purpose.

If the man God made you to be is only marginally related to the work you do, then why work? Justo could have used his inheritance to retire and nurse his illness. He could have spent his time and money building a golf course and then enjoyed years of early morning golf and leisurely afternoons talking sports and politics at the nineteenth hole. Should we pray to be rich so that we can pay other people to do the work?

Justo didn't seem to think so. Why not? Because he was a monk. The money he inherited was really God's money, and God called him to be a monk and build the church. Monks serve God and the church. If you feel you've somehow been wronged so you choose to disregard your vocation, or if you think you've served your time and can step away from the thing God made you to be and do, you may unnecessarily expose yourself.

Out of Position

Many years before David ascended the throne of Israel, God anointed him to be king. During the protracted period between the calling and the coronation, David faced obstacles and fought people who were bent on preventing him from becoming the man God called him to be. When he finally wore the crown, David continued to face enemies from without and within, so he continued to war for a long time in order to bring all things under his authority.

After years of going to battle, David reached a time when he felt others could go for him. Scripture tells the story:

> In the spring of the year, the time when kings go out to battle, David sent Joab, and his servants with him, and all Israel. And they ravaged the Ammonites and besieged Rabbah. *But David remained at Jerusalem* (2 Samuel 11:1).

When David should have been going to war and doing what kings do, he sat down on his leather couch and grabbed the remote to watch the TV programs he had recorded on TiVo. After catching the PGA tournament recorded from the previous Saturday, David grabbed a glass of tea and went out on the deck to soak up some late-afternoon sun.

No one in the houses below the palace expected the king to be home in the late afternoon. The women, including Bathsheba, assumed David would be off at the war with their own husbands, so Bathsheba probably thought little of bathing on the rooftop below the palace.

But King David was indeed home instead of where he was supposed to be, and that circumstance caused David to be vulnerable to something that would never have had access to him otherwise. The end result was that David stole a man's wife and then had the man murdered.

Paying the Price

God gives us a *thing*, and we are to pursue or live out that *thing* our entire life. It is who we are. When we ignore, discard, or miss our *thing*, we are out of position and exposed to our own weaknesses. We also affect the people around us.

When I was in law school I had to take a course in criminal law. Because I was in a part-time evening program, we had an adjunct professor who also practiced law full-time. Whether because of the workload of his practice or the rush-hour traffic I do not know, but our professor was always 20 to 25 minutes late for the three-hour class.

The man had a rather laid-back style and wasn't as intimidating as the other profs, and he never really grilled us in the typical Socratic style of teaching law. After lecturing for about half an hour he generally sent us on a break. Though he would call out a ten-minute time frame for the break, he invariably stayed out of the classroom twenty or more minutes himself, only to return to the same halfhearted style of teaching.

I don't recall anyone complaining to the professor or administration about the quality of his teaching or his style. Instead, most of us quietly celebrated because while we waited for the teacher to arrive or return from break we each worked on homework for the other demanding classes. In fact, his less-than-engaging style of teaching allowed the class of 60 people to do homework the entire three hours. We came to class overwhelmed but generally left feeling much more in control of the demands of the other classes.

In the thirteenth week of the 16-week criminal law class, I was working on homework when I suddenly had a chilling epiphany. As is common in many law classes, the only test the entire semester was the final exam. The grade we received on the final exam was the grade we received for the semester. The chill I felt came from the sudden realization that my professor wouldn't be constructing that exam. The exam would not be based on what or how my professor taught but on what we were supposed to know about criminal law.

The department chair would write the final exam, and he wouldn't give a rip about how late the professor was for my class or how little criminal law I was actually taught. Every person in my class would take an exam that had been prepared according to the assumption that we had been taught criminal law.

In a matter of seconds following that realization I was out of my seat and loading books into my briefcase. I excused myself as I passed down the narrow row of chairs and desks on my way out the door and to my car. I knew I would never learn criminal law from the teacher, so I had to teach myself 16 weeks of criminal law in three and a half weeks.

My professor was probably a great attorney, but he was not a great teacher. He was not even a good teacher. In fact, he was a bad teacher. Where was the good teacher? Perhaps the man who should have been *teaching* law was busy doing an abysmal job of *practicing* law. We needed a legal teacher but had none, so many people in that class who did not find another way to learn criminal law failed the class.

This experience helped me begin to realize that when a man is out of position, others pay the price. In similar fashion, the story of David made me see that when a man stops doing his *thing*, he produces the same result—others pay the price. Man's work is attached to his identity, and when man is separated from the *thing* he was made to do or be—or when he has no idea what his *thing* is—others pay the price.

Again, the penalty of Adam's sin was not work. Work didn't come into the world through the fall. *Sweat* from work is the consequence of sin, and that is because sin always takes our eyes off the task and off others, and it puts our attention squarely on our selves.

What I Do

What was so important about Adam's work? Was he the continuous gardener simply to keep him busy and out of trouble? No, nature was dependent upon Adam doing what he did. Some things can't exist until you rise to your challenge...until you cultivate and groom them...until you name them. Perhaps that is why prayers of confession often include these phrases:

Most merciful God,
we confess that we have sinned against You
in thought, word, and deed,
by what we have done,
and by what we have left undone.

Let's start by looking at our *thing*, and then we can look at why it may be a sin to leave our thing *undone*.

If I were to ask you to name your *thing*, chances are you would tell me what you do. But because your *thing* is related to your identity, it is first associated with who you are, and then who you are is applied to what you do. To understand your *thing*, you have to go behind what you do. Let me explain.

I have a friend who plays the guitar for a living. To be able to earn his living playing the guitar we can safely assume that he is very good at it. If you ask him *what he does* he will tell you he plays the guitar. But if you ask him *who he is* in the context of what he does, he will tell you that he is a musician. He *uses* the guitar to *do his thing*—be a musician.

I have another friend who moved to Franklin, Tennessee, to plant a church. Shortly after arriving in town he started a small business selling blinds and shutters because he needed to support his family. If you ask him what he does he will tell you he sells blinds and shutters, but if you ask him who he is in the context of what he does he will tell you he is a pastor. He sells blinds *so that* he can do his *thing*—be a pastor.

Quite a few years ago my family went through a very difficult time. For a variety of reasons my small production company faced a sudden decline in both projects and clients, so I had to close the company. The financial ripple was huge, and I needed to find new work. I had fairly extensive experience in several areas, but I couldn't find work anywhere on the employment spectrum. I interviewed for executive positions and seemed to be a leading candidate but heard nothing back. On the other end, the owner of the gas station looked me right in the eye and said he wouldn't hire me as the night manager of his small station because when I got back on my feet—which he was more sure would happen than I was at that time—I would leave.

We had to move out of our house, and the stress of the situation produced health issues. We went from a beautiful lakeside house with a small dock to a bedroom in the house of a wonderful older couple in our church. Many of our friends and acquaintances had no idea where we had gone, and we had no phone in our own name. My only income was the $120 a week I made leading worship at a church on Sunday. My wife and I felt as if we had fallen off the face of the earth.

Each evening we would take walks and try to figure out what to do. I would tell her about jobs I had applied for, and we would try to make sense of where we were and what we were doing. I felt as if I were in prison on one hand and totally scattered on the other—running in every direction seeking work.

You may understand how this feels and how it makes you question who you are. If I couldn't get a job, then who was I? When people asked me what I did, what could I say?

The woman we lived with was a spiritual well. She and her husband were also going through a difficult time, so she spent considerable time in her Bible each day before she left for work and then again at night.

Although she had her own issues and struggles, one day as we sat at her breakfast bar having coffee she looked at me and said, "I've really been praying for you, and I feel God has been telling me the same thing each time I pray. God keeps telling me that you are a herald."

I thought to myself, *Well, that's great, but did God tell you where a herald goes to find work? I know the classified ads pretty well, and I have yet to find a job listing for a herald.*

The word *herald* sounded weird, yet over a period of several days, I thought more and more about it. If God was indeed speaking to me through this wise woman, I needed to stop and think about what she said. Eventually I began to realize that *herald* wasn't first associated with what I did; God was telling me who I was. If that was true, then who I am should guide—inform and direct—what I do.

I began to study the word *herald.* I concluded that a herald proclaims or announces a message. He publishes or goes before an event to make something known. But more importantly, he delivers someone else's message. A herald carries the message of his employer, which in days of old was the king. If a herald announces his own message, he is no longer a herald.

The word *herald* suddenly connected a line of jobs in my past that included being a trainer, working in broadcast news, being a youth minister, and studying law. It took years to really understand the power of the word in my life, but that single word subconsciously began to direct me through and out of the valley time we were in, and with only a slightly higher level of awareness, it directed me toward jobs, education, friendships, and interests.

As I look back now I can see an absolutely clear path and how the thread of the word *herald* ties everything together. But I wish I would have had more clarity earlier in order to avoid a lot of anguish. I do know this: I am a herald. That is who I am. Right now I am writing this book and developing online programming for a Christian organization. That is what I do, not who I am. But who I am is inextricably tied to what I do. It's my *thing*.

Your Job

So what's your *thing?* Are you a teacher, a musician, an administrator, a leader, a helper, a tactician, a counselor, an advocate, an artist? Your thing may be associated with your job, but then again it may not. When it is, it makes job choices clearer, and it can infuse your job with more meaning. When it isn't, it can make a man feel off course, or think he has missed his life purpose.

Recently I attended a school function for my children, and in the course of the evening I met a man I'll call Brent. When our conversation turned toward work, as conversations invariably do, Brent said he owned and operated a small business. But he quickly added that he was really a songwriter. Since I was writing this chapter at the time, I was particularly intrigued by his distinction between what he was doing and who he was, so I listened closely.

Brent talked about all the years he spent trying to make a living in music—either playing or composing—but he could not do so. I discovered that Brent was just a few years shy of being 50 years old, and he admitted that he well understood the slim odds of making a living playing music at this point in his life. But he still hoped that his songwriting would pay off.

We shared the stories we had heard of famous musicians struggling for years, giving up, and then suddenly being discovered. Brent went on to recount the time his band *nearly* landed a deal with a record company, and the time a big-name rock band took his demo tape—only to apologetically return it five minutes later citing fear of a lawsuit for plagiarism. We talked about his friends who had one by one given up on the idea of making a career in music. Occasionally I heard in his voice the fatigue and skepticism of years of near misses and failure. At other times I could clearly sense his determination.

As we talked, the faces of people I've known over the years who had similar experiences floated through my mind. I wondered why it seemed so rare for men to do what they think they are supposed to do. By the time Brent and I turned our attention to the other people standing around us, I had almost decided to go home and delete this chapter.

As I told my daughters Brent's story on the way home, my oldest daughter reminded me of my auto-broker friend who felt God wanted him to be a pastor. My daughter and I recalled his decades-long struggle before he recently concluded that being an auto broker didn't preclude his being a pastor of sorts.

As I noted in chapter 4, my friend realized that God gave him success in his job of helping people buy a car so that he could also help and encourage certain customers going through particularly difficult times. Many of these people would never pass through the doors of a church. But doesn't God want to reach them right where they are? If every person called to pastor worked in a church, a huge group of people would never find spiritual help and encouragement.

How about Justo and his cathedral? Could he just walk away from his vocation as a monk because no one would hire him, so to speak? No, he could not *not* be a monk, regardless of what he did.

Then I remembered my own father. He worked in a lumber mill nine hours a day, six days a week until he was in his sixties. But each evening he visited people in the hospital, served on the board at the local rescue mission, and ministered to elderly people in the nursing home. He went anyplace he thought someone might need encouragement. If you asked him what he did he would say he was an electrician, but if you asked him who he was, he would have told you he was a pastor.

A friend recently told me about a grudge she held against her father most of her life. Her father worked the same job for more than 40 years, and every time he was offered a promotion he turned it down. Refusing the promotion meant the family had less money, but the genesis of the grudge was that my friend also interpreted it as a lack of initiative. How could her father not want to do more or to advance in his career?

As she continued, she confessed that she had totally misinterpreted her father's actions. Yes, refusing each promotion meant less money, but each promotion also would have meant more time away from home. Instead, her father chose to get up early every morning, lace up his boots, put on his work jacket, and do his job. But at the end of each workday he returned home to take his kids to their games, practices, and performances. He consistently put in his time at work and then quietly served his kids. So quietly, in fact, that his children didn't even realize what he was doing until they looked back afterward and realized how much different life would have been had their father's *thing* been his job. It wasn't, and her father knew that even if no one else did.

Till the Soil

That brings us to the essence of your *thing*. The common denominator in every man's *thing* is this: It is always about tilling the soil in someone else's life. It is about taking care of someone other than ourselves. That alone would separate us from animals.

Sure, animals take care of their offspring and even extend themselves on occasion to strangers. But mules don't aspire to the plow, and dogs don't spend time researching the best college for guide dogs. Yet millions of men have spent enormous amounts of time and money preparing to serve others. This happens even in cases where the man will not be able to make a living doing the thing he studies.

In the creation story in the book of Genesis, a couple of verses really help us see the importance of knowing and doing your *thing*. They give us a glimpse of how God sees you as a man and the value He assigns to becoming the man He made you to be.

> In the day that the LORD God made the earth and the heavens, when no plant of the field was yet in the earth and no herb of the field had yet sprung up—for the LORD God had not caused it to rain upon the earth, *and there was no man to till the ground* (Genesis 2:4-5 RSV).

This passage of Scripture states that part of the reason no plants or herbs were in the fields was that no man was available to till the ground. Without man to care for it, vegetation would either wither and die or become overgrown. When one plant is overgrown it crowds out other plants. Overgrown plants quickly become unhealthy because they lack the pruning necessary for new life to emerge and dead sections to be removed. The soil is compromised because certain plants pull specific nutrients from the soil, and if one plant dominates the soil, the soil loses its balance.

When my family moved from Chesapeake, Virginia, to Brentwood, Tennessee, we purchased a house that had been vacant for a year. We closed escrow on the first day of August, so the yard had been pretty much unattended the entire spring and most of the summer. The first Saturday morning in our new home my wife and I rose early to attack the lawn and landscaping. We were both in the middle of writing projects, and the weather report indicated the temperature would top 100 degrees outside later that day, so we thought we would work a few hours at the most.

The previous owners had planted a lot of nice trees, bushes, and flowers, but because no one had tended them they were all seriously overgrown. The flower beds and natural areas were full of weeds. The sidewalk that led from the driveway to the front door was barely passable because of the limbs and bushes that had grown up and over it. My plan was to trim them back, spray in a little weed killer, and stack the trimmings near the front right corner of our yard for the city to pick up.

Ten hours later, the edge of our lawn that bordered the street was piled with limbs, bushes, and trimmings about seven feet high, ninety feet wide, and ten feet deep. I think more trees, bushes, and plants were ready to be hauled away than remained in place. But what a difference! Now the house was featured, and the landscape complimented both it and our property, rather than our property looking like a jungle and the house a bungalow. A house and a yard need someone to tend them and to bring out the best in them. Unattended, they have no sense of place or purpose, and the beauty they were designed to display remains hidden.

The same is true for your *thing*. Your *thing* is intended to bring out the best in other people, to groom and care for them. You must do your *thing* if certain people are to see who they can be. Sometimes your *thing* is associated with your job, and sometimes it isn't. But even when it is, it may not be obvious. Let me get specific.

At this point you should see that if you are on a quest to be known, other people are too. I hope you also realize that certain people play a significant role in helping you discover the man God made you to be. Finally, God made you to do a certain *thing*, and that *thing* is not so much about *what* you do as the who you are to be. God did not place Adam in the garden to build structures and monuments or to manufacture clothing for high-end retail outlets. He placed him in the garden to care for and bring forth life.

Creation still depends on men to do their *thing*, and that dependency requires man to be active. This is confirmed in the New Testament book of Romans, where the apostle Paul wrote that creation is waiting in eager expectation for the sons of God to be revealed. Man's destiny is mysteriously connected to creation, as we see in Adam's responsibility to create an environment in which nature could thrive.

The curse on the ground after Adam's rebellion paints a picture of man and nature working against each other. But creation is in eager anticipation—like a head being thrust forward—straining to catch a glimpse of the man God has called you to be. It hopes that you will both discover and pursue your *thing* and that you won't be detoured or discouraged.

All creation desires a man who is willing to endure suffering and hardship for the sake of the cause in his journey toward full adoption as a mature son of the Most High God. All creation doesn't mean just plants and animals. It means *all* creation—the men, women, and children around you who need you to be who you are so that they can become who God made them to be. We are to till the soil of their lives and help them find a way to thrive.

Paul goes on to say that sometimes we aren't sure how to pray, and this uncertainty can be extended into our *thing*. We just aren't sure of our *thing*. Or even if we can begin to put a name to it, we are still unsure of how to do it for the sake of others. How do we do the Father's work? How can we overcome our weaknesses and give of ourselves for the benefit of others?

Because God anticipated these times of uncertainty, He has placed in us His very Spirit—the Spirit of God—who knows both our weaknesses and

God's purpose. The Spirit intercedes for us in the groans and deep sighs of our prayers. The Spirit knows our hearts and minds, and He intercedes on our behalf according to the Father's will for our lives.

Paul then assures us that as we lay down our positions and possessions to embrace God's *thing* for our lives, God will work everything out for our good. After all, His calling on your life—your vocation—came from Him. You didn't make it up. He placed it in you.

Bloated and Puffed Up

You and I have been called to nurture the life around us. Yet most of us spend our lives propping up our own self-image and investing in ourselves. We actually believe that others will value us because of our money, position, or education. So we spend enormous amounts of time and energy accumulating money and burning the midnight oil to earn that coveted prestige. For all the benevolent and sacrificial things we do, the bulk of our efforts are subtly focused on ourselves and the person we want others to think we are. We unconsciously puff up ourselves with our accomplishments, our knowledge, and our money.

The truth is that people value us because of the contribution we make into them and the effect we have on their lives. Our celebrity culture notwithstanding, people don't live to stand around and look at how great *we* are, how smart *we* are, or how much money *we* have. Voyeurism feeds no one. If all those people we live with, work with, and pass by every day—family, friends, and strangers—could put into words what they sense way down deep in their hearts they would say to us, "Looking at who you are and what you own means nothing to me until I see you use it to help me live my life and to be the person God made me to be. Please, don't just stand there...till my soil!"

For the past 40 years, every time I've heard the phrase *puff up*, I've had the same mental picture. When I was young, my friend Will and I were walking across a field by our homes when we stumbled on a dead porcupine. It was lying on its back with its quills digging into the soft dirt, and it must have been dead for some time because the heat had made it swell up like a balloon.

I don't recall why, but for some reason my friend Will had a screwdriver in his back pocket. After gawking at the dead animal and poking it with a stick for a couple minutes, Will grabbed the handle of the screwdriver and pulled it out of his pocket. He then pointed it high in the air above his head and in one swift motion he threw the screwdriver straight down and into the bloated belly of the dead porcupine.

The point of the screwdriver punctured the skin and plunged deep into the animal's stomach. Suddenly we heard a loud *swoosh* as foul-smelling gas escaped from the porcupine's belly.

If we spend our lives focused on what we own and the titles we earn, and if we think our *thing* is all about being admired for those things, our funerals will be the functional equivalents of a screwdriver being plunged into our bloated dead bodies lying in caskets at the front of a church. With a big *swoosh,* the personae of the man we wanted people to think we were is punctured, letting out the meaningless vapor we spent our lives pumping into ourselves. And then the foul smell of our bloated self will expose who we really were. We were men worshipping at the feet of the idol of ourselves.

Wheat and Chaff

God had a *thing* he wanted the apostle Peter to do, but Jesus also knew that Satan wanted to detour and destroy Peter. On the night before His crucifixion, Jesus told Peter that Satan had asked God for permission to sift the disciples as wheat.

Have you ever seen old pictures depicting the sifting of wheat? A worker stands in a hole and uses a tool of some sort—perhaps a pitchfork—to throw the wheat into the air. As the wheat rises into the air above the hole in the ground, the wind catches the dry chaff and blows it away while the heavier kernels of wheat fall back into the hole.

Satan was sure that Peter was chaff. When the winds of difficulty and discouragement came, Satan was sure Peter would blow away.

Jesus saw Peter as wheat. Jesus also knew that God wanted Peter to do a *thing,* so Jesus prayed—not that God would prevent the sifting, but instead that Peter's faith would not fail. He recognized that Peter would go through a time that would seem—even to Peter—that he had walked away from the faith. That he had abandoned his *thing*. Yet Jesus was so certain that Peter would prevail in the sifting that He said, "And when you have turned again, strengthen your brothers." Who do you want to listen to, the person convinced that you are nothing—just chaff in the wind—or the person who is certain you are a man of substance—that you are wheat?

Your *thing* is always about tilling the soil in someone else's life. It is about taking care of someone other than yourself. You must see those around you as wheat—your wife, your children, your friends, your boss, and your employees.

When you begin to see others as wheat—as something of value to be cared for—you will begin to understand how your *thing* is associated with producing fruit. Most people understandably focus on producing fruit in their own lives, but just as important is the opportunity to provoke fruitfulness in other people's lives.

At the end of His earthly ministry, but before His crucifixion, Jesus prayed this prayer on behalf of His disciples:

> I glorified you on earth, *having accomplished the work that you gave me to do.* And now, Father, glorify me in your own presence with the glory that I had with you before the world existed.
>
> I have manifested your name to the people whom you gave me out of the world. Yours they were, and you gave them to me, and they have kept your word…I am praying for them. *I am not praying for the world but for those whom you have given me,* for they are yours…While I was with them, I kept them in your name, which you have given me. *I have guarded them, and not one of them has been lost* except the son of destruction, that the Scripture might be fulfilled (John 17:4-12).

The apostle Paul wrote most of the New Testament books. Like a sheepdog herding the flock toward the home pasture, Paul admonishes, encourages, and instructs groups of people—Romans, Corinthians, Galatians, Philippians, Colossians, and citizens of Thessalonica and Ephesus—for whom he feels responsible. He also drills down into the life of two individual men in the books of Timothy and Titus.

Adam was to till the soil in order to produce fruit. *Adam* wasn't the fruit. His work released the fruit around him. You too are to enable and release the fruit in the lives around you. When you don't, you miss the mark. You have fallen short. You have sinned. You have left undone the thing you were to do that day.

> Most merciful God,
> we confess that we have sinned against You
> in thought, word, and deed,
> by what we have done,
> *and by what we have left undone.*

10

THE STORY

In the end your child will not remember
you for who you were,
but who he knew you to be.
ALBERT CAMUS

....

WHEN I ENTERED EIGHTH GRADE, all 600 students coming into the school that year were required to take a placement test for math during the first week of classes. For me, that resulted in being assigned to the pre-algebra self-study group. One of the first concepts we began learning was how to solve for x. But because the class was self-study, no one really said the point was to *solve* for x. I thought x had some static, intrinsic value. As the teacher would occasionally move through our small group in the dimly lit room off to the side of the main classroom she would lean into one of the students, work with her for a few moments, and then hoarsely whisper something like, "So then, x is what?"

The student would then look up at her and say, "Eight" or something like that. Everyone in the class seemed to know what x was but me. I became so frustrated with myself and intimidated by the idea that everyone else seemed to know what x was, that after a month of classes I asked to be moved down two full math levels. I was committed to going back to general math and discovering what I seemed to have missed over the past few years of math class—the value of x.

Well, I didn't learn what x meant that year, so when I went into ninth grade I enrolled in general math again. *It must have been the teacher,* I thought. *Surely high school will have better teachers.*

But we spent the entire year reviewing what I already knew, and the subject of x never really came up. Either I didn't explain my quandary to the teacher very well, or the teacher thought I was as dumb as wood, and explaining the meaning of x would be useless. I am too embarrassed to tell you how many years passed before I discovered that everybody else did *not* know what x was, but instead each person had to *solve* for x each time they approached a new algebra problem with x.

I've come to realize that other people fell prey to the same assumption. My daughter has a cartoon in her math book in which one bright young know-it-all girl emphatically states something like "X is usually eleven, and y is almost always five." Some people may really think they have calculated a universal value for x, but I suspect a great many others are afraid everyone else knows something they don't.

Rules of Life

I think many of us assume that everyone else knows the rules of life, but that somehow we missed the lesson called "How to Become a Man and Navigate the Straits of Life." We imagine a home self-study version must have been available too, because other people missed school or had a dad who was away a lot—or didn't have a dad at all—and they stilled learned the thing everyone else seems to know. Everyone, that is, except us.

Therefore, we go through life quietly looking for someone who will tell us who we are and how to live. Regardless of how old we get, we still seem to be looking for that particular man who will stand on the sidelines of our lives and give us the signs, the plays—those critical principles we desperately need to know as we play the unforgiving game of life.

You may not have put a name to this need or spent much time thinking about it. But for many it lies beneath the surface of their consciousness, and it is always on the lookout for that mentor. As I talk to men who have reached middle age, they confess that deep down they feel like they are still just boys.

I think we each feel the need for a credible man we can trust, a man who will challenge us and call out the person we sense lies deep within. Somewhere inside we sense we could really *be* someone if we could just get access to the person inside us. We need someone who will tell us the essentials of life, which may in turn be the key to releasing that person we really want to be.

Discussions of sports, politics, business, and religion are seldom without this unspoken ache. Well hidden within those conversations is an inescapable connection between the people in the news or story and the person we think *we* could be. *They* could be better because if *we* were in their shoes, *we* would be better. *They* are good because they are doing the very thing *we* would do if we were in their position. We are interested in them because somewhere near the center of our being lies the belief that we could have been there if only we'd had the chance. We could have been a contender, but either the person we trusted and looked to failed us, or no one was available to teach us the ropes.

The Hole

The hole in some people's soul seems to be so big it tries to suck in any potential mentor that comes close. I remember becoming personally involved in the life of a fine young man who worked for me several years ago. He was very talented, and we worked together as he was transitioning from his academic studies to his vocation. The process was not quite as easy or quick as he thought it was going to be, so I was privileged to counsel with him for a few months as he navigated the move.

The time came for him to move on, and while he was training the incoming employee who would be his replacement, he apparently made a comment to him about my brief role as a quasi mentor. Several months later, the new guy was in my office, and we were discussing his job performance, which was below par. He was agitated and frustrated, and at one point he made a comment about me failing as his mentor. I was taken aback.

My immediate response was to ask him what he was talking about. "When," I asked, "did we move into a mentoring relationship?" I proposed that he was out of line blaming what he perceived to be my poor mentoring skills for his poor performance.

As I watched this young man over a period of years, he systematically selected mentors, and then one by one publicly exposed what he perceived to be failures on their part. He made such a public scene about one of them that this man was required to step down from a position he had held for years because the young man determined his "mentor" had failed him in some way. What a huge hole he had in his soul, and in trying to fill it he sucked potential benefactors into his vortex. No wonder we struggle to find a role model, a mentor, a man who will be a father to us.

The Elusive Search

My dad was a good father, but he was busy, and we spent very little time together in my youth. He worked hard and was a man of character, but we never really sat down and talked about the path to manhood—about the principles of life. I realize now that by my early twenties I, too, was looking for a mentor of sorts. And although over the years I met many men I thought could teach me the ropes, those relationships never seemed to work out.

Several decades ago the *Los Angeles Times* devoted a series of articles to a man described as a business genius—a turnaround specialist who worked magic in the toughest of situations. The article suggested he brought out the best in the people working for him.

Interestingly, I had heard the same thing about him my whole life, but not in a newspaper. He was the uncle of one of my closest friends. This "guru's" brother and nephews told me stories of his success throughout my childhood, and years later—shortly after these articles ran in the newspaper—they had an opportunity to work with him.

I was very interested in business and had moderate success in a few companies of my own, so I was thrilled when soon after my friends went to work for their uncle, I too was given a chance to work with him. In the process, I secretly hoped to be mentored by one of the masters. Though my father couldn't mentor me in business, I was confident that this man would teach me the rules of life and groom me to be like him—a great businessman.

A little more than a month after I started working for him, I sat down at the same table in the restaurant at which I ate breakfast every morning. Following my daily ritual, I read the *Orange County Register* and then dutifully picked up the *Los Angeles Times*. As I opened the business section, a picture of my new mentor caught my eye. It was an article penned by the same person who had written so glowingly of him just a couple years before, but this time the headline touted scandal.

As I read the article a pit began to form in my stomach, and my breakfast lost its flavor. Just as had happened before in my life and would happen again several more times, my role model was stripped naked and then knocked off his pedestal by the very people who had placed him there.

Mentors are valuable people, and if you are fortunate enough to find a valid one you can learn invaluable life skills. But I've discovered that the role a father plays is unique. It is almost irreplaceable, and it can trump even the most powerful mentoring relationships.

Alexander Hamilton was the first—and many say the finest—Secretary of the Treasury of the United States, and he was arguably one of the foremost architects of United States capitalism. He is best known for his work on the Federalist Papers, a compelling treatise laying out the rationale for the proposed Constitution of the United States of America.

Alexander's grandfather owned land in Europe that had been in his family for centuries and was a very wealthy nobleman. His son—Alexander's father—could have lived a life of ease and spent his days in philosophical thought, but he eventually broke ties with this powerful family and set off to make his own way in the new country. Though he was very bright and well educated, Alexander's father was a terrible businessman, and he had contempt for the idea of making money. Further, if he decided something was right as a matter of principle—even if he was wrong—he would ferociously defend his position, often in a very hostile and demeaning way. Some say he charted a life course toward self-destruction.

Young Alexander loved his father, and he shared his passion for philosophy. In Alexander's early years, he and his brother would sit at the family table and discuss all matters of money and men. But when Alexander was about nine years old, his father abandoned him, and as I understand it, Alexander never saw his father again. Following his mother's death just three years later, Alexander and his older brother were forced to find their own way.

After many years of hardship, study, and sacrifice, Alexander found himself in the company of the Founding Fathers. One of his best-known mentors was George Washington. He became Washington's personal aide and confidant, a relationship borne out of trust and mutual respect. One could hardly find a better group of mentors than the men who helped establish our nation and write its constitution. With Alexander's mind, financial genius, and considerable influence, he made many men very wealthy, and he could very well have done the same for himself.

But like his father, Alexander seemed to believe making money was somehow beneath him. Consequently, he was never financially stable. Further, Alexander had his father's temperament and confrontational style, and these traits created a great number of powerful enemies.

Alexander had many fine traits, each one cultivated and developed through study, sacrifice, and the rarest of mentorships. He had influence and success far beyond that which most of us could even dream. But many historians argue that he was also opinionated, belligerent, and condescending to the point of self-destructiveness. He thought little of pushing things beyond the point of civility, and being wrong mattered little—just as with his father.

Though many divergent and long-brewing factors contributed to the confrontation that July morning in 1804, some historians believe that the values and traits infused in Alexander by his father set him on the path to an unnecessarily early death. On the banks of the river in New Jersey, Alexander Hamilton died in a duel with Aaron Burr over a series of political attacks that a more temperate man may have avoided. Hamilton's life illustrates that the principles and values established by a father in the early years of one's life, even if those years are few, have tremendous power to shape the character of a man and to constrict the potential of a great mind, even with formidable allies.

The Trail

In chapter 4 we talked about intentionality, about the way God has laid a path before us. I also suggested that in addition to an intrinsic path that we are inclined to follow, we also leave a trail. Our DNA, fingerprints, and interactions leave traces of us that forensic experts can follow. But whether we intend to or not, we also leave a trail that our children tend to follow, though in their minds they may be working very hard to avoid it.

If you don't have children or grandchildren, you may be inclined to skip this chapter. But I ask you to reconsider. Stick with me for a few minutes because you may find that some of the principles we discuss will help you better understand your own life right now and understand why other people do what they do. But first we must give due time to the incredibly powerful role a father plays in the lives of his children and grandchildren.

In January 1993, Roscoe confidently stood before a jury, certain they would find him not guilty of aggravated assault and terrorist threats. Roscoe's version of what happened that day in the park a year and a half earlier—his seventeenth birthday—and the prosecution's story were completely different. So, according to the *Atlanta Journal Constitution,* Roscoe rejected a plea agreement. He believed his ability to spin things his way, a talent that had helped him dodge the bullet many times before, would once again keep him out of prison.

As a child, Roscoe was a good student but a troubled kid. He was on the honor roll in eighth grade and took advanced math courses in high school. But newspaper accounts indicated that he also got into fights, sneaked out late at night to binge drink, threatened his girlfriend, and tried to overdose on pills. His mother was a junkie, and he had seen his father only a handful of times. Although his aunt warned Roscoe he was going to wind up just like his parents, newspaper accounts say Roscoe believed his path was far different than the one his parents had taken.

Roscoe had walked the thin line between mischief and criminal behavior for years, but his luck ran out that day in January 1993. The jury found Roscoe guilty and sentenced him to four years in prison. Following a series of unsuccessful appeals, he began serving his time in the fall of 1994.

The newspaper reported that one evening in May 1995, Roscoe was filing down the hall of the maximum-security prison with the rest of the prisoners on their way to dinner when he spotted a thin, older man leaving his cell to join the line. The man had a tattoo featuring a skull and a top hat on his forearm. Even though Roscoe had seen him only a few times in his life, he instantly recognized the man as his father. Roscoe successfully avoided his father, but he later reflected that perhaps his path and that of his parents were not so different after all.

Roscoe believed he was walking an entirely different path than his father did. How could a father he had seen only ten times possibly have an impact on his own life? Yet, if he was blazing his own trail, walking his own path, and making his own way, how is it he found himself a few men behind his father in the chow line of a maximum-security prison? I can't speak for Roscoe, but the two men's paths seem pretty similar to me. The consequences of following that path were brutal and long lasting, and they excluded or hindered Roscoe from opportunities and interests that would have otherwise been available.

Though Roscoe stumbled upon the realization that he was indeed on the same path as his father, other men readily embrace the ways of their fathers. For years now, sports enthusiasts have watched Peyton and Eli Manning independently recognize and embrace their father's trail. Archie Manning, a former NFL quarterback for the New Orleans Saints, had tremendous success in professional football and a reputation as a man of character. He was also well liked.

A few decades later, who appears on the scene but his son Peyton, a star quarterback for the University of Tennessee Volunteers and a tremendously successful NFL quarterback with the Indianapolis Colts in his own right. He too is known for his work ethic and character.

Archie had another son who followed the same path. A college football success and first-round NFL draft pick with the New York Giants, Eli is making his own mark in professional football as a quality quarterback and a man of character. As unique and distinct as Peyton's and Eli's skills may be in their shared profession, they are clearly following a trail their father blazed.

We too are blazing trails, and we too are following trails. Some men struggle with the realization that they somehow can't avoid the consequences of life choices their fathers made, while other men gratefully acknowledge the benefits that accrue to them by following their fathers' trail.

You Look like Your Father

Scripture tells about one event in Jesus' life in which He confronted His critics and adversaries—men who took great pride in claiming they were sons of Abraham, Isaac, and Jacob—by telling them they weren't like Abraham at all. Instead, they were like their father, Satan.

Jesus said, "You are of your father the devil, and your will is to do your father's desires. He was a murderer…When he lies he speaks out of his own character, for he is a liar and the father of lies" (John 8:44).

Later, when Jesus was just hours from crucifixion, He stood with Pilate before the frothing crowd. Pilate brought another prisoner out, and according to custom he offered to release one of the two men. Pilate told the crowd he would release either Jesus who is called Christ, or Barabbas, a convicted murderer and scoundrel. Pilate put before the crowd a subtle but extremely symbolic option: choose Jesus, who claims to be God's anointed, or choose Barabbas.

The Hebrew name Barabbas is derived from two words: *bar,* meaning son, and *abbas,* meaning fathers. The name then meant "son of your fathers." Here was a clear choice for the crowd—align yourself with your family. Will you choose the anointed one of God, or will you choose the murderer who is categorically the son of your fathers—the murdering children of Satan. Who is your father?

The book of Proverbs states, "Grandchildren are the crown of the aged, and the glory of children is their fathers" (17:6). The word *glory* can mean character, or how a person is known—the real you. That is why, when Moses asked God to show him His glory, God told Moses He would make all His goodness pass before him. God would reveal to Moses who He is. *That* is His glory. If this is so, then perhaps the proverb is also saying the *character* of children will resemble their fathers'. That's kind of scary, isn't it?

What Happened

You may have had a great experience being reared by a father who loves you, is committed to you, admits mistakes, and has taught an advanced course in "how to be a man" to his sons. That must be the case, because we see so many fine men out there, and it is virtually impossible—not truly impossible, but virtually impossible—to become that way without outside influence. For you, I hope this chapter will encourage you to stay the course in the lives of your household, be they children or other relatives.

But that is not the case for many men. This is not at all about assigning blame. It is about recognizing the inclination most of us have to follow our father's trail. Many of our fathers were busy trying to be the man they felt everyone wanted them to be, trying to follow or avoid the trail laid down by their father, or subtly trying to find someone to teach them the rules of life. They simply forgot that they, too, were laying a trail down for us to follow. Most men underestimate the incredibly powerful force a father exerts in his children's lives, and that the force of their own life will significantly influence that of their children whether they realize it or not. Think of the many books and movies in which children struggle with their father's failures, inattention, or judgmentalism.

We can easily move through life trying be what we think we are supposed to be, find what we are searching to find, or do what we are trying to do. In doing so, we can become so focused on things ahead of us that we forget what is behind. In the previous chapter we talked about your *thing*, and we saw that men need to find and do their *thing*. But how can we do our *thing*, influence our children, and also impact the world?

Some men are compelled to communicate God's Word to the world. These men truly believe their *thing* is to change the world, save the world, or evangelize their world. They sense they are called to preach. But I believe it was Saint Francis who said that we should preach at all times, and if necessary, use words. How can you preach without words?

Noah's world was a mess. Evil and self-centeredness reigned, and God was very disappointed in what He saw. So, God called Noah to build an ark and load into it a pair of every kind of animal. That is quite a *thing* to be called to do. And though I've heard sermons about Noah preaching to the people of his world up to the time the doors of the ark were closed, I really can't find that in Scripture. The closest reference to that concept I can find is in the New Testament book of 2 Peter, where the apostle Peter refers to Noah as a preacher of righteousness.

But the New Testament writer of Hebrews says that by faith Noah built an ark *to save his household*, and *by that act* he condemned the world. Noah believed God when God told him He was going to judge the world, and therefore Noah should build an ark. In the end, other than his *thing* with the animals, Noah was responsible for his own family. That's it. His influence was focused on his wife, his sons, and his son's wives. Just eight people went into the ark.

Noah preached by obeying God. He built the ark and saved his family from destruction. As the rain came, perhaps the people began to cry out to God saying they were innocent, and God was unjust in His punishment. "It's a tough world," they might have said. "There are too many distractions—no one can obey You. Our children don't even obey us, much less You!" As they rail at the perceived injustice of their plight and the incredulous demands God puts on them, God simply points to the ark.

"Impossible?" God asks. "Noah obeyed me and taught his children to do the same." God might have continued, "and he took responsibility to ensure that each of his sons and their families were safe." As the rain began, this was Noah's sermon, and not a word was in it. First and foremost, you too are responsible for your family.

Charles Stanley, pastor of First Baptist Church of Atlanta, has had an incredible, quantifiable effect on the lives of millions of people around the world. I know this because I've read many of the grateful e-mails from people thanking him for the powerful influence he has had on them personally. Millions of people watch him each week on television, listen to him daily on the radio, or connect with his ministry online.

But Dr. Stanley's father died when he was young, and his relationship with his stepfather was admittedly strained. The summer before he was going to college, Dr. Stanley spent one week with his grandfather, during which they spent considerable time talking. I recently heard Dr. Stanley speak as forcefully and passionately as I've ever heard him speak when he emphasized the effect one week with his grandfather has had on his life.

Dr. Stanley's grandfather was the pastor of a small church in rural Virginia, and he probably preached to fewer people in his lifetime than Dr. Stanley speaks to in one week. But during the brief period he spent with his grandson, he told him stories of his life, incidents he recalled, and the lessons he learned from them. The senior Pastor Stanley didn't hand his grandson a manual. He didn't make him recite a series of value statements. He told him stories of his own life and the lessons he took away from them.

Years later Dr. Stanley condensed those stories into a handful of distinct principles that he has used to guide his life for decades. He said that those stories and principles are more valuable to him than all the money in the world.

Truthfully, money can't buy life principles, and Dr. Stanley freely offers them up for everyone's use. But while they are considerably helpful and valuable to you and me, they will never possess the power for us that they do for Dr. Stanley. Something special happens when life principles are passed down from your own flesh and blood. Something in the experience is much more powerful than the words.

Interestingly, Dr. Stanley's son, Andy Stanley, is also a pastor. Both men lead churches ranked among the largest in Atlanta, and they impact people far beyond the boundaries of their city. In a recent sermon, Dr. Stanley said people occasionally ask him why he doesn't do a particular thing, start a specific project, or engage a certain cause. He responded by saying that when his grandchildren are each grown and each one is following God, he may consider it. But for now he is focused on his own household. Hmm...sound familiar?

God of Our Father

I've always been intrigued by the way God introduced Himself in the historical books of the Old Testament. He typically said, " I am the God of Abraham, Isaac, and Jacob." God may deal with individuals uniquely, but His introduction seems to indicate that He intends to deal with men consistently. He seems to be saying that He is the God of their fathers, and a man learns about God from his father and from his father's father. God is not an unknown or new force in their lives. He has left a record of who He is, how He works, and what He expects.

God revealed Himself to Abraham, who taught his son Isaac, who taught his son Jacob. Abraham's children had unique experiences with God, but Abraham provided a trail of God's faithfulness and his own godly fear. Even so, each man had issues with his father. Abraham was willing to sacrifice Isaac to God, which must have been quite a shock for Isaac. Abraham's obedience clearly established the supremacy of his faith over everything else, but it must have left Isaac's head spinning.

Further, when God reiterated to Abraham the promise that his wife, Sarah, would have a son through whom God would extend His covenant, Abraham was at least initially disappointed that Ishmael would not be the chosen one. After all, Ishmael was in hand while Isaac was just a promise. And though Abraham deferred to God's plan, Isaac certainly experienced difficulties as he grew up in the same house as Ishmael.

As we discussed in chapter 6, Isaac's own son Jacob also struggled with his father. Isaac had a favorite son, and Jacob was not him. Jacob ultimately had to wrestle with the agony of his father's agenda on one hand and the person he sensed God made him to be on the other. But each time Jacob interacted with God, he was reminded that God was the God of his father, Isaac, in the same way Isaac had been reminded that God was the God of his father, Abraham. Each of the children knew exactly who their father's God was.

A Change of Course

So, are you without hope? Are you destined to walk your father's path with no chance to alter or change it? Must your father's errors forever haunt you? Perhaps not.

Why does the "I am the God of Abraham, Isaac, and Jacob" mantra start with Abraham? What about Abraham's father? Does God start with Abraham by chance? Did God single Abraham out on a whim? After all, God appeared to Abraham (Abram at that time) in Ur of the Chaldeans and called him to go to the land He would show him, right? Perhaps. But there is a little more to that story.

Actually, Abraham's father, Terah, took his son Abram, Abram's wife, Sarai, and his grandson Lot, and left Ur of the Caldeans to go to Canaan. But Scripture says that when they got to the town of Haran, Terah settled there. He stopped. He was on his way to Canaan, the land destined to be the promised land, and he stopped. There he lived to the age of 205, and he died …still in Haran.

When the story continues, we read that God called Abram to leave the land of his fathers and go to the land of Canaan. But Scripture doesn't really

say that either. Instead, it actually reads, "Now the Lord *had said* to Abram."
He *had said.* When?

Once again, this is the Marcus version, and the Marcus version alone. But
here's what I think.

Why did Terah leave Ur to go to Canaan, the land to which God ultimately
called Abram? Why does Scripture say God *had called* Abram? Had God called
Terah? After setting out for Canaan, did Terah give up?

Scripture says Abraham believed God, and that belief was credited to
him as righteousness. How do we know Abraham believed God? Because he
followed through. He left Ur of the Caldeans and went to Canaan. What if
Terah actually went all the way to Canaan—would the "God of your fathers"
mantra have been, "I am the God of Terah, Abraham, Isaac, and Jacob"?

This is all conjecture, but I think it brings up an interesting question. Do
some men receive a call from God to do some particular thing—specifically
to command their children and their household after them to keep the way of
the Lord—but then give up, leaving their sons to receive the call and engage
the fight? Are some sons presented with an opportunity or obligation to pick
up the load and carry it?

The Witness

If someone were to ask your children who your God is, what would they
say? Can they tell who you worship by the way you live? Have you infused
them with an understanding of who God is, how He works, and what He
expects from you and them?

You probably know the story of Sodom and Gomorrah, and you may
know that Abraham tried to talk God out of destroying the cities if He could
identify a handful of godly men. God said He would relent from destroying
the cities if He found 50 men in them who were godly, then 45, then 40, then
30, then 20, then 10. Ultimately, only Lot and his two daughters were saved
from destruction. But before Abraham began to barter with God to save the
city, God made a very interesting and telling statement.

Scripture implies that Abraham believed that the three men visiting him
constituted a physical representation of God. As they were leaving Abraham

and beginning their decent down the hill, into the valley where Sodom was located, God said this:

> Shall I hide from Abraham what I am about to do, seeing that Abraham shall surely become a great and mighty nation, and all the nations of the earth shall be blessed in him? For I have chosen [known] him, that he may command his children and his household after him to keep the way of the LORD by doing righteousness and justice (Genesis 18:17-19).

The word *chosen* is the Hebrew word *yada,* the same word used in the Scripture, "Now Adam *knew* his wife, and she conceived." God seems to be saying, "I know Abraham. I will show Abraham what I am about to do because he is the man I will use to bear godly children. If he is to successfully convey to his children the principles for a blessed life, then he must also see the punishment for wickedness. It will sear an image of destruction into his mind that will ignite a passion to keep his children off the path of wickedness."

But seeing the destruction also takes a toll. It is a great burden to bear. Remember, Lot was commanded not to look back—he was not permitted to see it. His wife didn't obey, and she was immediately consumed by the consequence of exposure.

Some generations don't have the same fear of aberrant behavior as those who see its consequences firsthand. My mother watched the toll of drinking in her father, and she had a great fear of alcoholic beverages. She would not permit them in our house. I often thought she overreacted, but I didn't see the consequence. She did.

The woman who cuts my hair recently brought up how many people sit in her chair and tearfully speak of the devastation alcoholism has brought into their home. Some men abuse their wives, some divorce them, and others just walk away from their families because they give up the fight and give themselves over to appetite of drink. Seeing the price of wickedness—the wages of sin—tears a piece out of a person's heart.

Men today have seen the effect of fathers preoccupied with work and by their desire to "change the world." We have seen men destroyed by drugs, by greed, and by rogue appetites. We look to our left and our right and see men adrift…men who by all appearances are successful, yet who live as if their souls are in a cage.

We desperately wish to protect our children from the same plight, yet the forces they face are even more daunting than the ones we faced. How do we change our culture and still protect and prepare our sons and daughters?

God Knew Abraham

Interestingly, when God promised that all the nations would be blessed through Abraham, He said that He *yada* Abraham. Abraham was chosen, like Noah, because (1) Abraham believed God and then acted according to that belief, and (2) Abraham would command (instruct, lead, provoke, insist) his children and his household to keep the way of the Lord.

God chose Abraham because he *knew* Abraham, and He knew that Abraham would lead his household well. Regardless of all the faults and failures each of us experience, it is our absolute insistence that our household will be saved —evidenced by the way we live and the values we instill in our children—that will shape the generations who will ultimately bless the nations.

The Chance

Your father may not have cut it as a father. You may not have cut it either, but you can make a new start right now. You can recognize your father's trail and realize that you are following it. You can ferret out the good and manage the bad, and you can take responsibility to see that your children or grandchildren do the same. You preach your best sermon by getting your family into the ark.

A story is told of a man who had been hiking in the mountains of southern Montana in mid summer. He got turned around and couldn't find his way out, and one hot day led to the next with no food, no water, and no way out. He was dehydrated to the point of exhaustion when he stumbled on an old abandoned farmhouse in an open field. No one had lived there for a long time, but the man found what seemed to be an underground well with an old, rusty hand pump jutting out of the ground. On a table to the side was a dust-covered glass jar full of water sitting on top of a handwritten note.

The note said, "Pour the water into the top of the hand pump to prime the pump, and then pump real fast. Don't forget to fill the jar and put it back on the table when you are done."

The man couldn't tell exactly how long the place had been abandoned, but considerable time had obviously passed since this pump was last used. And though the water in the jar was hot from the sun, it was clearly drinkable. It was also the only water in sight. If the man poured it in and the pump didn't work, or the well was dry, or if for any reason he couldn't get the water out of the well, it could be over for him. Should he play it safe and drink the jar of water, or should he risk it all in a chance for a whole bucket of fresh water now and more water for those who might follow?

After considerable thought, he poured the jar of water into the pump and started to pump the handle. He pumped and pumped and pumped—nothing. Nearly exhausted and ready to stop, he suddenly thought he heard a faint gurgling sound. He pumped faster, but nothing happened. Suddenly he felt the pressure of the water kick into the handle, and as he pressed down again, the water began to pour out of the pump and into the bucket below.

I have to confess that when I was younger I wondered why God didn't take better care of my father. He worked his tail off, and I couldn't see any benefit to him for doing it. After a long day of work in the lumber mill, my dad would drag me along when he went to fix the television of an elderly couple who had no money to pay him anything but the money for the parts. Rather than being at home where I could play like most ten-year-old boys did, I was sitting on the floor of a small, cold apartment that smelled like sickness, watching my dad spend hours trying to fix a broken-down TV set.

On Sunday afternoon when my friends were outside playing, I was at a nursing home, where I had to sing or play my trumpet before my dad would preach a 20-minute sermon. Then we would spend 15 minutes going down the hall to visit the people too sick to get out of their beds to come to "the service."

Later that night, when my friends were watching *The Wonderful World of Disney*, I was at the Union Rescue Mission, where once again I had to sing or play my trumpet before my dad preached the requisite sermon that allowed the men in the small chapel to get a hot meal and a warm bed for the night.

I still remember the smell of the place and how glad I was to be done each night.

My dad always paid 10 percent of his income to the church, without fail and without exception. He truly believed that if he was faithful to God with his money, God would be faithful to him. But we were pretty poor. We didn't have much money at all, and it seemed to me that if God was going to be faithful, He better get busy doing it because my dad was having a pretty tough time making ends meet. Yet each pay period, my dad confidently wrote that tithe check, certain that his tithe was invested in the very thing God wanted it to be invested in.

The year my father died I was on staff at a church in California. The doctor told my sister that anyone who wanted to see my father before he died had better get there quickly. So I made arrangements to cover my duties at the church, piled my family into our old car, and set out for Oregon. During those last days as I sat around my father's bed, the thing he talked about over and over was God's faithfulness. He stressed the importance of each of his children and grandchildren getting along with and supporting each other. He had no money to pass down to us, and nothing of any real value. He spoke to me a bit about his concern for my mom. He told my brother and me that we could have his tools and the few books he owned—a handful of Bible commentaries and some books on electrical wiring.

The evening before he slipped into unconsciousness for the last time, he asked me to bring his wallet to him. It was very worn, and I could see that he had precious little money in it. My dad reached in and pulled out a folded piece of paper, which I quickly realized was a check. It was the very last check he wrote in his life, and the notation at the bottom read "tithe."

It was made out to me.

The Value of X

My father essentially had no knowledge of his father, so he was forced to battle demons about which he had no warning. Many times I sensed his restlessness, yet I witnessed his determination to persevere on a new road with little support. He faithfully navigated a life with very few material benefits, all the while choosing to serve some people in the nursing home and others at the rescue mission—people who had nothing to offer in return. Like Lot, I had not seen the penalty for living a self-centered and self-destructive life, but my father had. He wanted a chance to change things for himself and his children.

I recently cleaned out some drawers in my home office, and I discovered a worn old piece of paper. I opened it and saw it was a copy of that check my father had written to me back in October 1995. I realized that God's blessing on my wife and children, my job, my education—and even the very real sense that God is directing my life—is a result of my father's faithfulness. What would have happened if my father had given up in the hard times or focused on his own needs and desires rather than those of others? Where would I be if my father had not poured that jar of water into the pump to prime it?

On my forty-eighth birthday my eldest daughter gave me a gold box about ten inches wide, eight inches high, and an inch thick. It had a bow on the top and looked like a box of candy, similar to the ones from Godiva chocolates. On the front were written two words: "You Are…"

The box seemed too light to be full of candy. Yet as I opened it I half expected to see some sort of raspberry candy—my favorite. Instead I saw a bunch of little strips of paper. They looked like the paper you'd find in a fortune cookie, so I opened one and read it: "Fun." I opened another: "A good cook," and then another that read, "Relatively healthy."

I laughed at the last one and looked up at my daughter, who said, "Whenever you are unsure about who you are, just open the box. There are 49 of them—one for every year of your life, plus one that says '48' because you always think you are a year older than you really are." We all laughed about the week before my forty-seventh birthday when I realized I had spent the whole year thinking I was 47.

I then closed the box without reading any more. I wanted to sit down by myself later and read the things she had written. When I did, I was moved beyond words. I had in my hands a box of words that described the person my 14-year-old daughter saw as her father. What others said about me suddenly didn't matter so much—good or bad—because someone who knew the good and the bad wrote 48 words preceded by the phrase "You are." I could spend my life on the big screen, a Broadway stage, or the cover of magazines and never have anything more meaningful said about me.

You may have a wonderful, close relationship with your children, and they may have insightful things to say about you. On the other hand, you may have made a lot of mistakes in plain view of your family, and those mistakes may have negatively shaped who you are in their eyes. You may have even sidelined yourself or felt disqualified. But if you engage or reengage in the lives of your children, grandchildren, nieces, and nephews, you have a chance to change things.

I doubt that this is what Albert Camus meant when he said, "In the end your child will not remember you for who you were but who he knew you to be," but I think that in the end your family will look past your mistakes and failures if you will truly *know* them, let them *know* you, and tell them the stories of God's faithfulness in your life. You may not see those stories yet, but they are there. And you have yet to live many new stories.

In the end, the value of x is unique to your own equation. You may have a lot of work ahead of you to solve for x—to know your true value and to live out that value in the lives of your family. Nevertheless, the value of x is going to be shaped by the people closest to you and by the way they relate to you. Further, as in all math equations, x not only is affected by the value of the properties around it, it also affects each of those values as well. No one outside your equation can tell you what your value is. Only those certain people and the God who placed that value in you before time began can do that. How will you be known?

11

THE CORNER

The cream of enjoyment in this life is always impromptu.
The chance walk; the unexpected visit...the unsought
conversation or acquaintance.
FANNY FERN
....

In the early 1970s, Ken spent many hot days and long nights wading through the marshes and jungles of Vietnam. As members of the elite Army Rangers, Ken's small group of five men spent most of their time doing reconnaissance or patrol, and very little time at camp. That was just fine with Ken. He had always been a loner, and the four other men who made up his team pretty much maxed out his social skills. Thankfully, most of them were also reserved and aloof...deeply committed to each other, but in a distant, assumed sort of way.

On this particular day, Ken was the third man in line as the group of five trailed 300 North Vietnamese. The Rangers were totally unaware of a small group of enemy soldiers that had broken off from the 300 and circled back, ultimately placing themselves directly in front of the five Americans. Their first warning was the sharp *clack-clack* they heard a split second before the bullets hit.

Instantly the lead man was dead—shot in the head. The number two had been shot in the throat, and blood was squirting in quick, red streams from the hole in his neck as he desperately tried to cover it with his fingers. A bullet pierced the muscles, tendons, and joints connecting Ken's right leg to his hip, knocking him to the ground as a grenade exploded behind him. The explosion killed the fourth and fifth men and sent searing shrapnel into Ken's arm and shoulder. Then, for some unexplained reason, the attack group pulled back.

Ken was unsure why the attack stopped, but he was determined to use the brief respite as a chance to get away. Though the pain was excruciating, sheer adrenaline gave Ken enough energy to crawl toward some thick groundcover in a field a few dozen yards away, desperately trying to cover his trail as he went. The Ranger in front of Ken—the one who got a bullet in the throat— had stabilized himself enough to get the bleeding stopped. When he did, he realized the bullet had gone in and out, and in the process it had done very little damage. Within about 20 minutes of the attack, Ken had found a bush large enough to hide in, so the other soldier helped cover Ken up, and then he set off to get help.

No sooner was he out of sight in the trees to the southwest than about 100 North Vietnamese emerged—guns poised—from the northeast. They spent the rest of the day walking all around and in some cases over Ken, who was trying as best he could to *be* the bush. At nightfall many of the enemy soldiers left, but a couple dozen remained behind and set up camp.

By the third day the soldiers were still there, and to keep from screaming out in pain, Ken had torn off a piece of his shirtsleeve and shoved it in his mouth—and practically down his throat. Earlier that morning Ken heard an occasional helicopter circling at varying distances. Using the small, black mirror tucked away in his gear, Ken tried to signal the copters. This went on for several hours, and then there was nothing until mid afternoon.

About 2:00 PM a swarm of American helicopters descended with guns blazing, routing the North Vietnamese soldiers in quick order. Ken and the bodies of the three dead rangers were hoisted onto the copters and flown back to camp. On the flight back, as the medic was treating him, Ken was finally able to breathe a huge sigh of relief. In the moment before he collapsed from relief and exhaustion, one thing became very clear. Though Ken had always been a loner and he preferred being left alone, he didn't want to be alone that day.

As he reflected on his thoughts while buried in the bush, Ken became aware of a feeling stronger than the pain he had felt. It was an overwhelming fear that seemed to come from deep, deep within him, and he was finally able to give it a name: Alone. He didn't want to die alone. He didn't want his lifeless body lying in the jungles of Vietnam far from his home and family.

Alone

Recently our three-year-old cat had some sort of neurological episode that paralyzed his left side and nearly blinded him. We had him treated and worked with him for a month, but he was clearly getting worse. After talking to the vet, we all agreed to give him just a few more days to see if he would recover before we put him to sleep.

My wife and kids had to go out of town for four days, so I was left to monitor the cat's condition. During that time he was lying in a cat bed in front of the fireplace, and for three days he didn't move, although he was still alive.

After having been out of the room for about an hour, I walked in to discover that the cat had crawled out of bed and about three feet toward the door. I assumed he was getting better and was hungry or thirsty, so I got him some food and tried to feed him. But because he was paralyzed, about all he could do was lay his face in the bowl and then awkwardly lick his lips. After a couple minutes of this he pulled his head back and laid it on the floor. I changed his bedding, put him back into the bed, and covered him up.

The next morning I took him to the emergency vet. Shortly after checking him in, they called me back into the exam room and told me the cat's core body temperature was 90 degrees, and for comparison a temperature of 99 would be considered low. The vet said the cat's body was trying to shut down, so we agreed to put the cat to sleep.

As I waited for the vet to return, I suddenly realized that the previous day when the cat crawled out of his bed he wasn't looking for food or water. He was crawling away to die. Animals seem to instinctively want to crawl away to a solitary, secure place and die alone. My cat's instincts told him to crawl away, but I returned him to his bed, where he lingered, unable to die because somewhere inside he sensed that this was not the environment in which he should do so.

Instincts

Our instincts are the opposite. Few events create more unease than the thought of your own death. You realize that you must face death alone, yet you also *fear* that you will face it alone. Deep inside, you do not want to be alone at death, nor do you want to die in a place where no one knows you. As death approaches, we feel the need to resolve differences and to see our siblings, wife, or children once again. We need to know that someone is with us, in a sense holding our hand in this life as we reach out into the afterworld and try to take hold of a hand on the other side. We are between two worlds, and we need to be known on both sides. People recognize this need to be with someone at death, and we each sense the tragedy when we hear, "He died all alone."

We have seen the story of Jacob's early life in the book of Genesis. Later in his life, famine drove his family out of his homeland and into Egypt, where his son Joseph had become a powerful figure. As Jacob sat in his bed just days away from death, he surrounded himself with his family and called his son Joseph to his bedside. He told Joseph not to leave him in Egypt when he died. Jacob made Joseph promise to carry his bones back to the land of his fathers and to bury him there. He did not want to be buried in a land of strangers.

But if this is the case at death, then perhaps it is also the case in life. I think men today face two conflicting emotions: the *need* to be alone and the *fear* of being alone. A man desires to make his own way as a unique person. He wants to establish himself apart from others and apart from his parents, but somewhere inside he senses a quiet fear of being alone. We have moments of intimacy with our wives and then moments of isolation. We have seemingly conflicting duties to be with our kids and yet the duty to provide for them, which takes us away from them. As times passes, we settle into the patterns of life and become accustomed to a deep sense of estrangement.

It's not that we really *want* to be alone; we just don't know how to *not* be alone. The December 20, 2005, issue of *USA Today* quoted Professor Peter Nardi as saying that in the past, men were much more expressive, but in the late nineteenth century, men started to distance themselves publicly from other men because of the influence of Freud and discussions of homosexuality. Whether that is true or not I do not know, but I do sense that we men feel somewhat alienated from others, which in a strange way makes us at odds with ourselves.

Do you ever feel that little by little you are walking away from yourself? That the man you've become—regardless of how great you may be—is a shadow of the man you were made to become? Deep inside, do you subconsciously harbor qualities and interests that you can't seem to access or bring to the surface?

Perhaps the opposite is true. Do some things about you make you cringe? Do you fear that one day you may be exposed for all your failures and weaknesses, for things that you work daily to cover up and camouflage? Do you hide your true self behind an elaborate scheme of smoke and mirrors?

This is what alienates you from friends, your family, and ultimately yourself. Not the *things* you hide, but the fact that you *hide.* You are hiding the man God made you to be because that man is fragile. He isn't fragile because he is a weak person; he is fragile because he has been hidden and neglected. Given a chance to mature, he can be a warrior, philosopher, and king. Said another way, that man could be strong, be wise, and be in a position to protect those under his care. Instead, this man lives his life all alone, hiding in the caves of your soul.

But even in the caves of your soul, God is with you. Further, you don't have to find your way out of the dark places alone. I want to offer you three distinct pictures, each representing a different model or perspective of friendships. I hope these pictures provide a glimpse into the varied roles unique friendships can play and the significant value they can bring to your life. The pictures are not associated so much with who you are as with seasons of your life.

As you read, think about your friends. Do you have friendships you don't even realize you have? Have any men in your present or your past played a significant role in guiding you through a difficult time? Who are they? Where are they now? One or two men around you may be poised to play a major role in your life, yet you don't even see them. Or perhaps some men have called out the man God made you to be, but you were so fatigued from the fight of life that their voices never really got through. Who are the men who carry your story?

Picture One—Mighty Men

Scripture tells us that Saul, Israel's first king, was strong, personable, and a leader. He was the kind of guy we all want to be. We know this because when Israel petitioned God through the prophet Samuel for a king, they did so because they wanted to be like other nations. The wanted someone to be their icon—a man who would represent the best of who they were. Someone both admired and feared. So God picked Saul, a man heads and shoulders above all other men.

Saul filled this role for quite some time, but eventually he became so concerned with being the man everyone else wanted him to be—and thought he should be—that he chose the voice of the crowd over the voice of God. Saul never really had a very high opinion of himself, and perhaps he wasn't quite sure what the crowd saw in him. When God ultimately rejected him as king, Saul continued to look and act the part of king, but he was constantly tormented. His turmoil was likely a symptom of an inner fear that people would see through his persona, or maybe it was the loss of what could have been, had he just been the man God made him to be.

About this time, young David entered the picture. Though he was not quite the imposing physical presence Saul was, David was also the kind of guy most of us would like to be—strong, handsome, and a leader. At first, Saul really took to David and made David part of his royal court. After all, David had killed the giant, Goliath, with a sling and a stone. His abilities could take the focus off of Saul's weaknesses. Further, David had a way with music that could assuage torment. When things went from bad to worse in Saul's mind, David played music to soothe Saul's troubled soul. I can imagine that David reminded Saul of himself…of the kind of man Saul thought he could be or at least could have been.

But the very traits that made Saul partial to David began to make Saul hate and fear him. Saul could see God's favor on David, and though Saul was a good man, Scripture says God saw David as a better man. Like looking in a mirror that had broken in his own hand, Saul could sense God's favor on David. If Saul had realized Samuel had already anointed David as king of Israel, he would have killed David immediately, which indicates that perhaps Saul's troubled soul perceived his own death sentence before his mind could put a name to it. For David's part, he carried a secret he shared with only a handful of men, and none of them could have any way of knowing David would not attain the throne for many years. First, Saul had to die.

As David served Saul in battle, his popularity grew. And as his popularity grew, so did Saul's jealous rage and hatred of David. While Saul's staff tried to keep David out of the way, only David could comfort Saul's torment. Long story short, the very thing that drove Saul crazy was the only thing that could bring him peace. Finally, Saul tried to kill David, so David headed for the hills, where he spent years hiding from Saul and living in caves.

David's Three

When David fled from Saul he had nothing. On the way out of town he managed to acquire Goliath's sword, the weapon David confiscated after he cut off the giant's head. Shortly thereafter he headed to the hill country with its caves. And here, "everyone who was in distress, everyone who was in debt, and everyone who was bitter in soul [restless] gathered to him" (1 Samuel 22:2). There were about 400 men.

Remember, God viewed David as a better man than Saul, but David was hiding in the caves with a bunch of malcontents. Do you ever feel that the person God created you to be can't seem to overcome the man you've become? You feel alienated from the majority of the people around you, and the men drawn to you seem to be as pathetic as you feel. But something is afoot. In the midst of your restlessness and that of those around you lie the seeds of victory. The man of valor within you is about to find his way.

David and his group began to rise against the enemies of the land. They went to work to defend the food supply of their families and neighbors, and in doing so a very interesting thing happened. Out of the hundreds in David's band of men, a small group emerged in David's life. These 30 warriors who rose to the top were the best of the men in the company—David's mighty men—and they become men of renown. But out of this small, tight, and formidable group of men who lived together, ate together, and fought together, three would ultimately be known as "the three."

These three men may not have been the life of the party or had the best political connections, but they had a very unique bond with David. For instance, when enemy troops separated David and his men from the water in the town of Bethlehem, David made a comment about his desire for a drink from a particular well by one of the city gates. These three men then risked their lives to break through enemy lines, fill a cup with water from the well, and bring it back to David.

The Bible records some of the exploits of a few of the other 30 warriors who were known as David's mighty men, but it adds this line: "But he did not attain to the three." In fact, of one man Scripture says, "He was the most renowned of the thirty and became their commander, but he did not attain to the three."

Altered Expectations

In the handful of years between the time I moved from hands-on media production to the academic world, I developed a unique relationship with three men. We all served together on a board of elders at a small church in the Saddleback Valley area of Southern California, and we were each working through our own set of philosophical and theological issues which—unknown to us at the time—would shape the direction of our lives for years to come.

It started with a decision to have breakfast together each Saturday morning at 7:00. We were each somewhat different and had unique styles of interaction, but gradually we began to deal with some pretty deep spiritual issues. Our discussions at the small table in the restaurant commonly lasted until 11:00 AM or longer—more than four hours. Sometimes a few other men would join us, but typically two or three of us from the original group would still be there, deeply engaged in conversation, hours later.

With these three men I felt I could do something I hadn't been able to do before: I could speak actual heresy. I didn't know it was heresy until I said it or until one of the three repeated back to me what they heard me say. I just said something I had been thinking about. While it remained in my head I really didn't understand it as well as I thought I did. I realized I needed to take it out of my head, so to speak, and hold it out at a distance to look at it.

While I held it out at arm's length and admiringly beheld what I believed was an incredibly profound philosophical proposition, one of the guys would give me a look as if to say, "Marcus, that is the stupidest thing I've ever heard."

Sometimes it was. Other times their response and input helped me transform a completely whacked-out thought into something worth consideration. It was one of the greatest gifts I could have received. Most men would have smiled and nodded—all the while thinking what the other guys actually said—leaving me alone in my flawed thinking. Even if they said the very same thing as my three guys, I would have been embarrassed or defensive, neither of which would have moved me forward in my journey toward the man God made me to be.

I had a high level of trust with these three men, based on several factors, including time and a shared experience. Each of us was either in a time of transition or unknowingly about to enter one. We each also had similar yet unique philosophical and spiritual perspectives. And, we were each responsible to the church we served.

Lastly, we all brought something to the table. Other men may have been smarter, richer, and more talented. But these men had specific traits that I needed in my life right then, and they were willing to put themselves on the line for me.

These three mighty men supported me in my business and then helped me work through the financial ripples of closing that same business. They were with me in the uncertain days when a doctor thought my wife may have miscarried our second child. Then, sitting together on a deck in a backyard one evening, I told these men about a dream I had a few days before in which I truly felt God told me to move to Virginia and pursue my doctoral degree. In a unified voice they confirmed my sense, and then each did whatever he could to support that transition.

The following year would bring an end to that particular season we shared together, but our experience changed my level of expectation for relationships. I didn't need to find a group of men; I needed to find certain men. But the place to discover these men likely would be in a group of men.

Ultimately, only a handful of men—six in all—were closely connected to David and influenced him in particular ways at particular times. These include the three mighty men; the prophet Samuel, who first anointed David as king; the prophet Nathan, who confronted David when he sinned with Bathsheba and had her husband killed; and Saul's son Jonathan, who was David's closest friend as a young man. Each of these men knew David uniquely and impacted him significantly.

Picture Two—the Corner

I really enjoy watching team sports like football and basketball. The symmetry of individuals working together for a common goal in a team sport is both inspiring and fun to watch. But my family and I also watch individual sports, and the skill required in one-on-one competition and the associated isolation of the individual is equally compelling. When surfing through channels, my wife and daughters often demand I stop on figure skating or gymnastic competitions. But I always hear a subdued grumbling sound if I happen to stop on a golf tournament. Still worse is the revolt I suddenly experience if I happen to click to a boxing match.

Recently I was comparing team and individual sports, and I realized that the differences are not as clear-cut as they seem. Yes, the weight of the competition in individual sports is significantly focused on one person, but that person still has a team. His team is just much more behind the scenes than in football and other team sports. For example, in auto racing, the driver and the pit crew work together to form a racing team. A more subtle example is boxing.

For some reason the boxer's corner has always interested me. Could you imagine a heavyweight title bout in which a fighter spends three minutes in virtual hand-to-hand combat and then returns to his corner to wait for the next round all alone? No, in the few seconds between rounds a trainer is adjusting and tuning the fighter's brain, while a cut man works diligently to fix wounds that could otherwise leave the fighter vulnerable. Someone else may be rubbing taut muscles, trying to loosen them up.

Experts agree that, in many fights, what takes place in the corner of the ring in those 60 seconds can be the difference between winning and losing. This is true not just in tightly matched championship bouts, but also in contests that should be more easily decided due to the skill of one of the fighters. Running a corner is a science, and the men who serve the fighter in the corner are professionals. Everyone from the cornerman to the man holding the spit bucket impacts the fighter and enhances his chances for winning.

Tim Hallmark has been a trainer for 30 years. He has trained people for practically every sport, but I think he has a unique insight into the boxer's corner. He was the conditioning trainer for four-time heavyweight champion Evander Holyfield. In the middle of Holyfield's first championship fight, he was getting tired, which was understandable because Evander had never had to go more than seven rounds.

Between rounds, Hallmark looked Holyfield in the eyes and said something like, "He's counting on you quitting. I know you hurt, but I also know that you're in the best shape of your life. Push yourself…you *will* get a second wind." Holyfield did, and he went on the win the fight.

Hallmark said his words were effective because Holyfield knew Hallmark had been with him every day. Hallmark went in the ring with him and left the ring with him. In certain ways, Hallmark knew Holyfield better than Holyfield knew himself. Additionally, Hallmark knew Holyfield well enough to use certain words. He knew the trigger words for Holyfield—the words that formed connections and painted descriptive pictures.

Because of their history, a cornerman can say to a fighter, "Remember when we did this and it worked?" or "Remember when you did that, and you got slammed?" He might say, "We've worked too hard to get here for you to lose this fight to this guy."

Hallmark says the key is trust. The trust allows the man in the corner to help the fighter see things he cannot see. But the fighter has to listen. When a trainer says, "You've got to change this," the fighter will choose to listen or not. If he doesn't, the cornerman might say, "You can't do what you're doing and win this fight."

In your own life, the men in your corner can say, "Listen, I'm with you to the end, but if you continue to cut corners…" or "If you continue to see that woman…" or "If you let that sin remain in your life…"

Sometimes the men in our corner can see down the road better than we can. The cornerman knows boxing, he knows the fighter's style, and he can help the fighter judge his effectiveness. He can say, "It may not look like it's working right now, but if you keep throwing that jab, it will work." The conditioning trainer knows whether the fighter is in shape or not, and he has more insight than the fighter into whether he will get a second wind.

But you will also need a cut man. This guy may not have known you all that long. In fact, your cut man may have no connection to the other men in the corner, but he is in there because he is very good at what he does. He is a utility player, brought in for a specific fight and to play a specific role. He is *so good* at what he does that he is qualified to stop a fight and preserve you for another day and another fight. But he also has the skill to handle a nasty wound and keep you in the fight, which is often the difference between winning and losing.

My friend Brian is a television producer. I was in his office recently talking about boxing and the men in the fighter's corner. I was writing this chapter at the time, and our conversation began to transition to our own lives, to our own desire as men to be contenders in life. We talked about the need for certain friendships—for men who play specific roles in the fight called life. As we were talking, Brian's whole body became energized as he began to list the men in his corner and the role they play in his life.

Brian said, "My father is my cornerman. He encourages me and gives me clear advise, but he does it in a way that keeps me calm and focused. My friend Bobby is my trainer. He keeps me on track, challenges me, and pushes me to be my best. But he will also get in my face and tell me I'm blowing it."

As he continued, Brian said, "Now, my brother, he's my cut man. When I'm in trouble or really struggling with something, my brother just instinctively knows what to do. And he just does it. No lectures, no whining—he just jumps in and fixes it."

Then he paused for a minute, and in a very grateful tone he said, "But Charlie would carry the spit bucket. That's a tough job. Think about it… carrying a bucket for a guy to spit out the water he just sloshed around in his mouth. Charlie is always there for me, doing anything I need him to do."

Who is in your corner? Who are the men in your corner who know you better than you know yourself? Who will help you see who you are and tell you the truth—particularly when you don't want to hear it?

Newspapers reported that near the end of a very close fight, heavyweight champion Michael Moorer's trainer, Teddy Atlas, looked Moorer in the face and said this:

> Do you want me to trade places with you—is that what you want? Listen, this guy is at the end of his rope. There comes a time in a man's life when he has to decide if he wants to live, survive, or win. You're doing just enough to keep him away from you and hope that he leaves you in peace.
>
> You're lying to yourself, but tomorrow you'll be crying. You're lying to yourself, and I'd be lying too if I let you get away with it. But tomorrow you'll be crying. Do you want to cry tomorrow? Then don't lie to yourself.

Have you reached the time in your life where you have to decide if you are going to live? Will you just survive, or will you win? After years of battling the forces of life, you are understandably tired. You have been chased around the ring by a four-time heavyweight champion, or by King Saul, or by whatever personal demon you have been fighting for years. And, for the sake of argument, you've done okay. Yet the face of the man God made you to be has grown so dim, you aren't sure if it really matters anymore.

A year ago I was there. I had this book outlined and in proposal form. I had the first couple of chapters written, and it was in the hands of a few publishers that were considering the book. Honestly, it is very difficult to get a book published anymore, and the odds against it happening are staggering unless you are already published or you have a built-in audience. I was not already published outside academia, and I had no built-in audience.

About this time, my wife was reading a new book by a rising star in the Christian book market, and she began to talk about what a great book it was. As she read each chapter she raved more and more about it. Because of her work, she receives a lot of books to review. Well, the combination of the great books already out there and the sheer volume of great books coming out had me against the ropes. I didn't realize how depressed and defeated I was feeling until I sat down with my friend Jonathan for lunch.

Jonathan and I have known each other for decades, and we have been through many things together, so I kind of let it all out to him. I told him I realized what a stupid idea it was to write a book and that I had no business wasting the paper. I wasn't looking for pity; I had just come to realize that great books are already out there, and great men are writing them. I had finally faced the facts: No one needed me to write a book.

Jonathan reads a great deal, so he is familiar with the book market and very savvy in both business and ministry. I truly expected him to come clean and admit I was right—in a nice way of course. Friends are used to friends coming up with ridiculous ideas, and about that time the idea of writing this book seemed like an idea Kramer on the NBC sitcom *Seinfeld* would have.

I never expected Jonathan's reaction. He pulled his head and shoulders back, and with a shocked look on his face, he just stared at me for a second. Then he leaned toward me, and with a voice and tone that sounded almost authoritative he said, "You have to write this book. This is a great book. What are you talking about?" His certainty kind of broke through the fog of doubt and discouragement. His voice made me answer the bell for the next round. I was still in the fight.

Picture Three—Six Men

I have a very distinct and irreplaceable relationship with a few men. I can talk about who I am and what I'm doing, and they will laugh with me, moan with me, and pray for things I ask them to pray for. But although I may have spent years telling them stories, laughing, and sharing my struggles, somewhere along the line I stopped telling them who I was, and they started telling me who I am. Generally, they don't say very much at all. Their few words have the effect they do only because of the people saying them.

Sometimes I go through times of introspection, trying to figure out why I do certain things or why I don't do certain things. Some event or struggle brings a character, personality, or capability trait to the surface, and I try to work my way through the issue. As I process this in my own mind, I may have an epiphany—a light will go on, and I suddenly see a trait or behavior pattern I hadn't seen before. When this happens I feel pretty smart, as if I'm my own psychoanalyst who had some major breakthrough into such an obscure and hidden area that the revelation was almost poetic.

As I share this insight with one of these unique men, almost without exception they look at me as if to say, "Yeah, well, where's the news?" It's almost as if I'm the last one to know who I am. I no longer have to be the person I think they want me to be; I just need to spend time with them to rediscover the person God made me to be. They have no agenda. They use no double-talk. They don't try to spare my feelings...nothing shades or compromises the value and impact of their encouragement. I am a better man because of the *me* they challenge me to be.

The Weight of our Casket

My friend Victor has never been at a loss for friends. He's not the life of the party guy or the kind of guy who entertains you all night with stories or jokes—though he could. Instead, he is just a quality guy, and other men get to know him easily. Perhaps that is why so many people attended his fifty-third birthday party.

I have to tell you, the party was incredible. It was a formal event at the country club, and I would venture to say that close to 200 people attended. Now Victor is not a wealthy man, so this party must have really set him back quite a bit of money. So why he would choose his fifty-third birthday to throw such a big bash?

Victor's fifty-third birthday party was significant because no man in his family has ever reached his fifty-third birthday. Not his father. Not his grandfather. Not even his uncles. No one. Victor is the oldest of four brothers, so reaching that mark also meant a lot to them. But Victor has a second hurdle, one that his brothers don't face. He has muscular dystrophy.

Victor and I had lunch together when I was in California a few months before that birthday, and our conversation got around to the search for six men who really know us and who will someday put their shoulder to the weight of our casket. As we talked, we realized that friends—even good friends—don't necessarily "carry our story."

Victor is a successful businessman, a priest, and a seminary professor. He has many, many friends. But we both realized that in the large group of talented and loyal friends, a handful of unique men are bound to us in an almost mystical way. These men may never meet each other until the day of our funeral, but they share one common trait: They each serve as a mirror that allows us to see ourselves, and they tell us who we *can* be. And at the end, they will stand and tell the world who we really were—not for the benefit of those in attendance, but for our benefit. We need our story to live beyond us.

But think about this: If these six men will tell your story at your funeral, then can't they do the same while you are alive? Why wait until the end to hear who you are and to help others do the same? What a valuable treasure is right in front of you! They are a critical part of the antidote to your sense of restlessness and estrangement.

12

THE HOLY GRAIL

But the sweet vision of the Holy Grail
Drove me from all vainglories, rivalries,
And earthly heats that spring and sparkle out
Among us in the jousts, while women watch
Who wins, who falls; and waste the spiritual strength
Within us, better offered up to Heaven.

from *The Holy Grail*
BY LORD ALFRED TENNYSON

....

ONE WARM APRIL EVENING IN 1987, a small group of friends and I decided to do something completely out of the ordinary and embark on a game night. The group included both girls and guys, so to be fair we decided we would start off bowling, then play miniature golf, and then try the new game that just opened in a building by our office called laser tag. We were all pretty competitive, so we agreed that the scores in each of the games would be combined to produce an overall score, and the person with the best overall score would be the undisputed champ. It seems pretty silly now, but back then it felt like a chance to be a kid again.

Not to brag, but things started off well for me. I hadn't bowled in years, but I ended up with what I think were two of my highest scores ever. Next, I could do no wrong in miniature golf. Regardless of how many golf balls were in my way, I was in the zone, and my putts were amazing. As we left the bowling alley in Irvine and hit the 405 freeway on our way to play laser tag in the north Orange County area, I was quietly confident I would win this meaningless competition with ease. No one was close to my score.

Laser tag was a brand-new thing then, and it sounded like a lot of fun. After paying our fee, we each received a gun that was attached to a plastic vest with encased electronic targets, which we dutifully strapped on so that they laid on our chests and backs. We then donned the plastic electronic helmets that truly made us look ridiculous.

The earpiece inside the helmet made one sound if you hit your target and a different sound if you were hit by someone else. If you were hit, your gun wouldn't work for ten seconds, which I guess was the penalty for getting whacked.

We stood by the doors, patiently waiting for our turn to enter the 12,000-square-foot warehouse filled with obstacles and pseudo structures used for cover as "warriors" battled it out on their way to the exit on the opposite side of the room. Our group was in the front of those waiting, and about 20 more people behind us were ready to enter when we did. Being the paranoid strategist that I am, I figured that the people in line behind us would immediately start shooting me in the back the second I entered the gaming area. So as the doors opened, I set aside what little dignity I had left, crouched down, crawled a short distance, and then ran for cover. I didn't give my little group of friends a second thought. They were now the enemy.

I didn't do the drop and roll move, but I permitted myself to do pretty much anything else I felt I needed to do to win the game and hence the championship. In my mind's eye I could see me accepting the award as I laughed about how silly and meaningless it all was, all the while thinking, *It may be silly and meaningless, but I still won.*

I moved with stealth speed and shot anyone who was in my way as I jetted across the giant warehouse toward the exit door on the other side. As I pushed open the metal doors and emerged into the little waiting area, I was amazed that I had gone all the way through the maze and had not been shot one time. Further, I must have set some sort of record because no one else in my group—or in the group of people behind me as I entered—came through the exit doors for as least ten minutes after I did.

As small clusters of people exited, they were all laughing and talking about how they ambushed each other, or how they ganged up on one guy the whole time so that his gun only worked two or three times. They were each sweating, but they went on and on about how much fun they had. As I looked at the target on the front of one of my friends, I saw a small "hit" counter that had kept track of the number of times he hit someone else's target. His number was something like 212.

Ah, I thought to myself. *That's how we discover our scores.* I looked at mine, and it said 18.

Oh well, I continued to myself, *just wait until they factor in the time it took to go through the course and out the exit door, and the fact that I didn't get hit by someone else even one time. That's where I smoked them.*

Well, I shortly discovered that there was nothing awarded for whisking through the game unscathed. My score was so abysmal that I dropped to fourth place in the competition.

The Journey

As we discussed in chapter 1, life is a journey with a purpose. We don't meander through life marking time until we exit.

In this journey, many of us spend the bulk of our time unconsciously focused on ourselves and on "making it." Without realizing it, the hour or so we allocate to spiritual issues each week becomes most closely associated with ritual, reading the signs of the end times, or engaging in just enough spiritual activity to ensure we don't miss heaven. Prayer is a comfort and Scripture a guide, but spirituality can feel increasingly disassociated from the day-to-day process of life. We can *feel* as if they are two distinct and separate parts of our existence.

I don't know about you, but at times I have felt that I was missing the whole point of life, which just magnified the restlessness I was struggling with. Oh, I tried to be a good person and to grow in my spiritual knowledge, and with varying degrees of success I attempted to manifest some semblance of the fruit of the Spirit in my life. But it seemed as if I were managing some meaningless carnival dime-toss game while the Super Bowl or March Madness was going on just around the corner. I knew a bigger game was out there, but

I just couldn't see it, or figure out how to get a ticket. I couldn't get into the *real* game.

Neither our spiritual lives nor the here-and-now lives we engage every day are to be lived the way I played laser tag. We cannot simply try to get to the other side without offending God or others. Why? Because our spiritual lives and the here-and-now aspect of life we engage every day are not mutually exclusive. Instead, they are inextricably linked.

God put our spirits in bodies for some honorable reason, not just to showcase our failings. What father—most of all what loving God—would do that to his children? And while our human nature tends toward selfishness and rebelliousness, if God has reconciled our spirits to His and placed His own Spirit in us, we must somehow be able to become, as the apostle Paul said, more than conquerors. If so, where is that man?

Holy Grail

A couple of weeks ago in a conversation with some men at work, someone brought up the movie *Monty Python and the Holy Grail.* Immediately guys started quoting lines about weight ratios of coconuts and African swallows; "Bring out your dead...he's *almost* dead," and "Oh that...why, it's just a flesh wound." Suddenly I couldn't get the song "I've Got a Lovely Bunch of Coconuts" out of my mind.

When many of us think of the quest for the Holy Grail, we think of Monty Python. Others think of the legendary King Arthur. For some, the phrase is a synonym for something unattainable: "His search for a perfect wife is a search for the Holy Grail," or "Their search for time travel is a quest for the Holy Grail." In other words, the quest for the Holy Grail is associated with folly, folklore, or fanciful dreams. But what *is* the legend of the Holy Grail?

Because of the work of nineteenth-century artists, most people think of the Holy Grail as a chalice—in particular, the cup used by Jesus Christ in the Last Supper. The word *grail* comes from the Latin word *gradalis,* which is associated with a dish in the shape of a large deep bowl that is used either to serve a meal in courses or to serve separate entrees together in one big dish.

The legend of the Grail is most closely linked to a man in Scripture named Joseph of Arimathea, the man who asked Pilate for Jesus' body in order to bury Jesus in his own tomb. Some people think Joseph of Arimathea may have also owned the house in which Jesus celebrated what we know as the Last Supper. The Holy Grail was supposedly the bowl in which the Passover lamb was served. Legend purports that Joseph of Arimathea used that bowl to gather the blood of Jesus as he took Him from the cross and wrapped Him in cloths for burial.

One version of the story has Joseph of Arimathea imprisoned in Jerusalem during the persecution of the early church, and that version states that during his imprisonment, Christ appeared to him and gave him the Grail. That bowl, the one that nourishes both soul and body, provided food for Joseph each day through his years of imprisonment. The Grail, then, is the vessel of eternal sustenance. It is a holy cornucopia or horn of plenty.

The legend then claims that upon his release from prison, Joseph fled Jerusalem with the other Christians, and he brought the Holy Grail to England, along with the Christian faith. The Grail was then guarded by Grail keepers—or Fisher Kings—in a far-off castle.

The quest for the Holy Grail was undertaken not for the chalice or the bowl itself. Though of immense historical value, and hence a nearly priceless market value, the Grail was nearly worthless in comparison to what it contained: the blood of Jesus the Christ.

Historic Christianity believed the blood of Christ held His soul and divinity, and all variations of the Christian faith—Coptic, Orthodox, Catholic, and Protestant, have sung about the power of His blood. Some "plead" the blood of Jesus over themselves and their families in a way reminiscent of the first Passover. Most observe or celebrate the blood of Christ in the Lord's Supper, the Eucharist, or Holy Communion. What could be of higher value? What could be a more noble purpose? What could offer more hope than to lay hold of the very blood of Christ? It is the pearl of great price, for which a man gives all he has.

But in the mythological tale of the quest for the Holy Grail, not just any man could seek the Grail. Only the man who had been purged and had demonstrated his obedience to God could approach the Grail.

This is the rub. Some men initially see the quest as something they can do to gain heaven. They subconsciously see it as a shortcut to salvation, a way to *earn* a place in the heavenly realm. But any man who engages the quest thinking it is a shortcut quickly discovers that securing the Holy Grail is not quite as easy as he supposed. In fact it seems quite impossible. For that reason, many men who set out on the quest will turn back. The journey will prove too much for them.

So what does the mythological tale of the quest for the Holy Grail have to do with your quest to be known? Everything, for they are one and the same.

The Distant Castle

The reason I say that your quest to be known is tantamount to the quest for the Holy Grail is this: Regardless of how modern and sophisticated the culture we live in becomes, nothing is more formidable or more rewarding than to find the Holy Grail—to know that you are fully known by God. We may think God is only concerned with our finding that place—the destination—but I think God is *just as* concerned and involved with the journey itself. He is as interested in how we move through the game of laser tag as He is about our exiting the door on the other side.

The quest for the Grail is a quest to *become* something, not to own or do something. Not understanding this, men sense the quest in diverse and futile ways. Some seek extreme sports. Some seek to know and be known by woman after woman after woman. Some seek knowledge, some wealth, and some power. But all of these merely represent our grasping for the answer, our struggle to find the path that will move us toward the true quest that lies in the depth of our soul. We continue to hear a voice calling from the hidden and unexplored areas of our being.

In the tales of the Holy Grail, the Grail is kept in a castle or a temple at the top of a mountain in a far-off, almost mystical place. In your own quest, the grail you seek may also seem far-off and distant. And more often than not, the search for this grail will drive you into unknown and uncharted areas of your own soul. As forbidding as that sounds, if you try to avoid the quest or find an alternative route, you will invariably reach a dead-end or loop back to the doorway of your true quest.

In the television sitcom *My Name Is Earl,* Earl concludes that the reason his life is so messed up is that he has bad karma, the result of years of selfish living.

He decides that the only way to change his life course is to go back and fix all the things he has done wrong. So one day he sat down and made a numbered list of his offenses. Each episode, then, features one or more of his attempts to purge himself.

When faced with the reality of who we are or who we're becoming, many of us desire to set things straight. Some people try to follow Earl's path—they want to go back and fix it all. But as Earl discovered in a recent episode, sometimes that just isn't possible.

In this case, Earl had previously promised to take his kids to a particular theme park, but he had consistently blown them off. The day Earl determined to cross the broken promise to his kids off his list, he discovered that he could not do so because, when Earl and his boys arrived at the theme park, it was closed—permanently. There was no going back.

In the midst of his exasperation, Earl's kids just looked at him and said, "It's okay, Dad." Then they told him that sometimes you just have to forgive the people you love, even if they've really messed up. Then they said, "We forgive you."

Earl wasn't seeking forgiveness; he wanted a do-over, but in this instance a do-over was impossible. But isn't it interesting that the thought of forgiveness never occurred to him?

Earl's path leads backward to his past. He is trying to change who he is by undoing previous wrongs. But we can't always do that. Instead, we should seek forgiveness and make restitution where we can, all the while realizing that trying to undo our wrongs does not make us right. You cannot undo your wrongs and call it even because the process of doing wrong has changed you. Further, it has alienated you from the person from whom you seek forgiveness, and also from God. You need to be reconciled to God through Christ before, or as part of, the quest. But, forgiveness is not the grail. It is not the destination.

The better path is a forward path leading to your future. You must find the man God made you to be. As author Madeleine Grace might say, the quest is a journey toward the awareness that Christ is in you, living in you. This quest leads you through the process of being known, both in and through the life of certain others, which is what this book has been describing to this point.

Your quest is formidable. It is a challenge. But your entire life is truly about discovering and being the man God made you to be. You are to know yourself as best as you possibly can, and you are to help certain others—your neighbors— to know themselves. In doing so, you quiet the internal restlessness. And as you love others, you begin to love yourself. At some point in this process you will find that with a joyful heart and a disciplined spirit, you love (desire, know) the Lord your God with all your heart, soul, mind, and strength. And as we saw earlier, the man who loves God is known by God.

One day, your journey will bring you to a place where you catch a glimpse of a castle in the distance—the place you believe the grail must lie. As you begin the ascent up the mountain of God, you become aware that *the man you had become* no longer lives. Instead, as the apostle Paul wrote, Christ lives in you. That is when you discover that *you* are the grail.

Jars of Clay

You have probably never seen yourself as the grail, and the suggestion itself may seem absurd. But let's follow this idea for a few minutes.

If you are the grail, then the body and blood of Christ lies within you. You carry Christ with you every moment of every day, everywhere you go. In the earlier part of his ministry, the apostle Paul wrote, "We have this treasure in jars of clay, to show that the surpassing power belongs to God and not to us" (2 Corinthians 4:7).

Paul goes on to say that we are always carrying around in our bodies the death of Jesus, *so that* the life of Jesus may also be manifest in our bodies. In this life we are always being given over to death, *so that* the life of Jesus may also be manifest in our *mortal flesh.*

Now, I understand that we live our lives in spiritual covenant through the blood of Jesus—His death. His blood on the mantle of our lives, so to speak, causes spiritual death to *pass over* us. But Paul also sees a direct effect on our human existence. Although we are dying every day, the death of Christ is impacting the life we lead in the here and now. It is changing us from the inside out. The presence of Christ on the inside can influence and ultimately change the person that walks through this life. People should perceive us differently as the death of Christ produces new life in us.

If that is the ideal, why is it not the real-life experience of so many people after they are reconciled to God? We are provoked to seek God because of mounting disappointments with life and with ourselves. When we give our lives to God, we secretly want immediate resolution to the internal churning and the dissatisfaction—we want to change.

But we discover that we have a hard time putting off the old self. Our experience with God is not changing us as easily and quickly as we desire. Further, now that the Holy Spirit of God is within us, we see our failures even more clearly...and painfully.

We don't really doubt that our reconciliation to God is complete. After all, we believe Christ carried the cross of our shame and died for our sins. We believe His kingdom can and should come. We hang on to the faith because we know it is true. But for some reason, we are still restless. We still haven't found what we're looking for. We become disillusioned with the day-to-day demands of life and our inability to rise above our failures, and the believers around us also seem to struggle with life. We want our faith to change us—to have an impact on our culture and our community. Yet our search sometimes seems futile, so we unconsciously relegate both the fruit and the utility of our salvation to the afterlife and to times of crisis.

The Grail

I think that deep down many of us become disappointed with the Christian life because we don't really know how to access what we sense is there. We read stories in Scripture, as well as historical biographies, of men radically changed by God in an authentic and almost enviable way. We want to *be* men of God, but we really don't know how to *become* men of God.

Jesus said that if any man is to follow Him, he must take up his own cross. He must sit down and count the cost. Jesus warned us in the Gospel of Luke that we should not start to build a house and then stop, because if we do, people will mock us. And they do, don't they! We tell people around us about the great thing God has done for us and how He has changed us, and then a year or two later those people see that we have given it up. We become an eyesore in the neighborhood, a half-finished house that leaves both ourselves and our families vulnerable.

Why? Because we don't *pursue* the grail. The apostle Paul wrote to men like this in his first letter to the Corinthian church. He said, "I could not address you as spiritual people, but as people of the flesh." Why? Because they are pursuing the things people of the flesh pursue. They are behaving like any other animal. An animal focuses on its need, its status, and its desires.

The kindling of our spiritual flame doesn't give us spiritual powers to perform natural deeds. It gives us supernatural powers—spiritual powers—to perform supernatural or spiritual deeds in pursuit of the needs and desires of the spiritual man.

After telling a lame man that his sins were forgiven, Jesus saw the cynicism of fleshly religion in the eyes of the men who had turned spirituality inside out. So then Jesus asked which was harder—to tell a lame man to stand up and walk, or to tell him his sins are forgiven. Then He told the man to get up and walk, not just for the sake of the lame man, but also so that those who misread the spiritual needs of people would *know* that Jesus had the ability to forgive sins.

How do you know which is the greater problem, the inability to walk or the sin and unforgiveness a man feels inside? How can a man of mere flesh and blood truly know the needs of others?

Only the spiritual man recognizes that God placed in a man the need to be known, and that it is this need that far outweighs any physical or natural need. Think for a moment about the man who is so lonely he has no appetite. Or the child who refuses to eat because of the grief she feels for having lost her parents—the only people who had ever cared for her. Even if she does eat, those around her may comment that her spirit is wasting away.

Certainly some people cannot sense the deep spiritual need each man has because of their own overwhelming natural hunger. They may live in an impoverished country with a government that stands in the way of food distribution. Perhaps that is why on the day of judgment, Jesus will tell some people who spend all their time casting out demons and amazing other people with their spiritual powers that He doesn't *know* them. He will continue, "I was hungry...I was sick...I was alone...I was imprisoned...I was naked... and you did nothing."

But the spiritual man on his quest for the grail is disciplining and training his spiritual powers to recognize and address the issues that keep people from seeing their real need. As heavyweight trainer Tim Hallmark said, "Life is for the conditioned." Therefore, when humanly possible, we remove the obstacles to people's understanding of the real need. We feed them. We cloth them. We give them medicine. We care for them. *Then* we go beyond those things, and "we destroy arguments and every lofty opinion raised against the *knowledge* of God" (2 Corinthians 10:5).

The spiritual man redeems and gives life to the mortal flesh. We use the body into which God has placed our spirit to accomplish what Christ Himself would accomplish if He were in our shoes in the flesh. We seek the mind of Christ so that we can pursue and discredit the institutions and philosophies that stand in the way of God, and that raise themselves up against every man's need to know and be known. Our life is no longer about *defending* who we've become. Instead, our attention shifts to *becoming* the man God made us to be.

Significance

What kind of grail are you? In ancient times, grails were very common and were used every day for all kinds of meals and occasions. But the quest on which the legendary King Arthur's knights set out was not for just any grail. Their quest was for the *Holy* Grail.

Near the end of Paul's life he wrote to his protégé in the book of 2 Timothy that a great house contains some vessels of gold and silver, but also some of wood and pottery. Some vessels are for noble use, and others are for everyday use. Clearly, each of these vessels is still in the house. They represent people who are all in the kingdom. But he goes on to say this:

> Therefore, if anyone *cleanses himself* from what is dishonorable, he will be a vessel for honorable use, *set apart as holy, useful* to the master of the house, *ready* for every good work (2 Timothy 2:21).

Paul goes on to describe to Timothy some key points in becoming a vessel of honor—a holy grail. Then, in the following chapter, he talks again about the vessels of *dishonor,* about their traits, lifestyle, and motivations.

He ended by saying, "But they will not get very far, for their folly will be plain to all" (3:9).

Earlier Paul had written a similar thing to another church in a passage talking about the work we do in the lives of other people. He said that we each do many things in the course of our lives, some valuable and some meaningless. But at the end of the day each person's work will become clear, whether it is a work of value—represented as gold, silver, and precious stones—or a work with no long-term significance—represented by wood, hay, and straw. Only works of value will survive.

When I was very young, my family lived in what used to be military housing that had been converted to apartments. They were clean and affordable, and because a lot of kids lived there, the summers were fun. The low cost also allowed my grandmother to live next door so that we could watch over her.

I was in the eighth grade when my grandmother died. In the months that followed we began to look at houses, and I was particularly excited about a brand-new housing development on the outskirts of town.

My dad saw things a bit differently. Although he agreed that the model homes—and the few that were already constructed—looked great, he was concerned that the speed at which the houses were constructed would make them show wear very quickly. He felt the builder hadn't given the ground enough time to settle and that he had not chosen materials that would hold up well.

I had no idea what he meant, so I continued to press him to buy the one we all liked. But my father wouldn't budge. We ended up buying a small home with much less aesthetic appeal in a different part of town. It looked like an ordinary home, while the one I liked—and my father dismissed—looked like a house the Brady Bunch might live in.

By my senior year of high school we had sold the house we had purchased four years earlier and moved to a different neighborhood. The house we sold was still an ordinary house, but it looked nice, and the neighborhood was very clean and appealing. In the process of looking for a new home we drove through the neighborhood my dad had previously rejected. He had been right. Time had revealed the quality of the material and the labor, and the verdict was not good. Not only did the particular house I liked look terrible, but the entire neighborhood looked that way.

Junk attracted junk, and the poor quality of construction made a place for poor quality of life. The entire subdivision had the feeling of a transient, poverty-stricken tenement. I'm sure no one planned on the micro-community turning out as it did. But the builder certainly chose the quality of his material and labor, and he made a decision about the kind of homes he wanted to build.

Would the builder spend his time and resources building a smaller house that would endure? Or would he build something that *seemed* better—that *appeared* to be of high quality—but that would quickly deteriorate after the sale? He may not have made quite as much money building a quality home… initially. But quality people who produce quality work tend to be recognized and called upon for more important work over time. In the end, a builder is honorable or he is not.

This is similar to the point Paul is making in 2 Timothy. The context of Paul's letter makes it clear that the vessels in the great house could choose what they were made of, and how they were used. So how did some become gold and silver wine goblets on display in the china cabinet to represent the wealth and greatness of the owner of the great house, while others were Dollar Store cups used in the bathroom for mouthwash? The quest made the difference.

It still makes the difference today. Our quest for the holy grail—the quest to be known and to help others do the same—is the path that leads to a quality life that has been molded into the image of Christ. The other path—on which too many men trudge along out of ritual, boredom, fear, or ignorance—leads to insignificance. The common path is a path on which men try to escape from the struggle. The noble path leads men to engage the struggle. So again I ask, what kind of grail are you?

In the last book of Scripture, the book of Revelation, Jesus dictates seven letters to seven churches in the first century, and the apostle John records these letters. In five of the seven, Jesus starts His discourse by saying, "I know your works." In one of the other two, He commends the recipient church for its faithfulness, but He still goes on to express concern about what they are *doing,* or how they are doing it. Jesus then lays out a brief course of correction to the people in those churches, and He ends with an interesting challenge.

Each and every time, Jesus ends by saying, "To the one who conquers..." and He goes on to state a unique reward. Evidently, making it to heaven is not enough. We need to conquer. We need to live today. Said another way, you don't have to die to be dead.

At the end of our lives, we will realize that the things we thought were important years earlier, and the things we thought we *should* be doing, are nothing compared to knowing Him, being found in Him, and seeing the effect of Him living through us in the lives of others. We will realize that other people are better because they encountered Christ through us, and in doing so they saw themselves and began to glimpse themselves through the eyes of Christ.

Begin

In the legend of the Holy Grail, knights who are weak in their faith or whose beliefs were in error could not seek the Grail. Only the bravest could approach the Grail. However, the ancient story also makes it clear that those who had previously begun the quest, but for any number of reasons turned back, may yet again undertake the quest. The legend further speaks of the unique nature of each man's quest, and the grace God gives to each man according to his ability to pursue the Grail. It is your unique quest. It is a noble quest. It is a priceless quest. It is the only quest.

13

THE BEGINNING

When you know what you're doing, you don't get intercepted.
Johnny Unitas (1933–2002)
NFL HALL OF FAME MEMBER

....

GARY AND STEVE TALKED BIG the entire trip to the cornfield. This was their fourth time to maneuver the maze of cornstalks, and the two boys made a bet with each other that whoever came out second would buy lunch for the one who came out first. When they arrived at the field, their parents paid the fee and arranged to pick them up four hours later.

They had heard rumors about something unusual with this particular maze. No one who successfully navigated it would tell its secrets, but the smirk on their faces revealed both the challenge and the personal reward. As the boys entered separate entrances into the tall stalks of corn, each was confident he would emerge the victor.

The corn was high and the day was young, so the sun gave nothing away. No one in the maze could tell east from west. Gary played to his instincts and previous experience, and he moved quickly through the maze. His friend Steve was more cautious and plodding, looking for signs and carefully choosing each turn and path. Surprisingly, both boys exited the course at about the same time. They were even more surprised when they discovered they were back at the start of the maze, exiting where they had entered.

Baffled but amused, Gary and Steve once again plunged headfirst into different openings and set about to conquer the puzzle. This time both boys adopted an aggressive strategy, and once again they emerged at the entrance. After the third time with the same result, the two boys hesitated and just stared at each other, unsure how to proceed.

As they stood there, they saw two other boys about their own ages exiting another entrance. One of the boys was excitedly telling the other that he knew exactly how to reach the far end. He was sure he had seen the right pathway, but he passed it up because he was trying to find his friend.

Gary and Steve quickly asked if they could follow, and the boy who was so confident seemed pleased to be asked to lead this small group of explorers. He said, "Sure, follow me!" and headed off into the path to their left.

The four boys moved quickly up one row and across another toward their chosen path. About an hour and a half had passed since Gary and Steve arrived, and the boys could hear more and more cars pulling into the gravel parking lot. The sound of those cars provided a clue that the boys were moving farther and farther from the entrance and closer and closer to the far side, which held the only three exits to the maze.

They were no more than six feet from the other side when their path made a hard left turn and traveled for about 30 feet parallel with the edge of the field before making another hard left. As the boys made the turn, they could see the straight and narrow row ahead that ran the entire length of the left side of the maze all the way back to the start of the course. None of the boys ran. They just silently made the long journey back to the beginning.

Once back at the start of the maze, each boy concluded that the other boys were idiots, and each took off in his own direction once again, only to reemerge one by one at the start 15 minutes later. This wasn't funny anymore.

The parents of the two other boys, the ones Gary and Steve had met earlier, arrived a short time later. After they left, Gary and Steve purchased a beverage from the concession stand and sat down at a small picnic table. As they drank, they watched and listened. Many people entered and reemerged just as the boys had, but a few others reached the far side.

As Gary and Steve listened, they could hear people yelling out clues and landmarks to friends and partners. In their own excitement and the thrill of competition, they hadn't really heard anyone around them as they each moved through the maze. They had heard noises and voices, but they hadn't really heard what the people were saying.

After finishing their drinks, the boys set out once again, but this time they were a little more methodical. Gary took a path on the right, and Steve took a path just a little bit to the left of Gary. As they walked, they exchanged information. At times they walked together, and then one would decide to go one way and the other another. In addition to yelling out to each other, the boys began to listen to the people around them. Gary, although pretty shy, was fairly strategic. He decided that as he encountered other people, he would ask them questions about their progress.

About 40 minutes later, Gary's path took a hard right and then another hard right. Soon, he was a considerable distance from Steve. Steve stopped for a few minutes and thought about going back to try and pick up Gary's path and lead him back to where they were last together, but he decided against this and kept going. After making a left turn, Steve's path went to the right, made two more right turns and a sudden left, and Steve was out. He made it.

After waiting about ten minutes, he concluded that Gary must have caught one of those one-way trips to the beginning, so he decided to start back. About that time he looked to the left and saw Gary exiting the maze with a huge smile on his face.

The Beginning

The morning I started to write this chapter I was reading the newspaper and saw a picture of a corn maze. When I did, I suddenly remembered Gary and Steve's story and thought about how much it relates to life. For all the progress you make in life, do you often seem to circle back to the beginning? I know that I have felt that way many times.

But I guess that makes sense because, as I mentioned in the early chapters of this book, God placed in you a desire to be known, and each time you move away from that quest, God will bring you back to it again and again. He may not take you back to the beginning, but once you engage the quest He will loop you back each time you stray from the process. As you get older, those loops will get shorter and shorter.

If you have never begun your quest, my guess is that you have probably experienced feelings very similar to those Gary and Steve had each time they exited where they started. Your existence can begin to seem futile, and you feel frustrated because you aren't experiencing the life you sense is just beyond your reach. A sense of insignificance may grow stronger as you discover all paths merely provoke a restlessness, which agitates you.

But if you have read this book this far, I suspect that the idea of being known as the path to significance is getting clearer to you. You may not yet fully *buy* it, but my guess is that by now you at least *see* it, and you are seeing it everywhere, in everyone, and in everything. So are you willing to try it? As you consider this, let me briefly restate a few things we discussed in this book.

First, the reason you are restless and you struggle to live a life of significance is that the quest is already in you. It will continue to churn until it is engaged, and it will reject all other paths. Second, you cannot complete the quest by yourself. You need certain other people, and you must know how to recognize them. Third, the quest to be known is in every other person around you. They may not know it, but you do. Therefore you have unique access into them, and this knowledge will allow you to help them, even though they may never put into words just what you did that made such an impact. Fourth, your task in this life is to till the soil in other people's lives—and most often, certain other people. Money, fame, or power will never give you the kind of satisfaction and significance you will find in doing your *thing*. Lastly, the purpose of this life is to allow you to mature into a fully functioning child of God—a son. Richard, a pastor and friend, likes to say, "You reap what you sow. God planted His Son because He wanted to reap sons."

Engaging the Quest

As you begin your quest to become the man God made you to be, confirm that you are aiming at the right target. Talk to God and then listen. You start in prayer, where you tell Him that you really want to know Him and rediscover the man He made you to be. Then you listen. One way you listen is by reading Scripture, including Psalms, Proverbs, and the apostle Paul's letters such as Roman and Philippians. As you read, occasionally stop and listen. I assure you, God talks. You just have to learn how He talks to *you*.

Being teachable is also important. By that I mean that you must be involved in a church where God can speak to you through biblical teaching.

But you must also do some very personal things. You need to recall your earliest years. How did your family view you? What positive attributes did they see in you when you were young that they don't see as much anymore? Pieces of you are still back there, waiting to be recovered.

What about you concerned them? You need to know about personality traits and tendencies that were troublesome in order to understand why others responded to you then—and respond to you now—the way they do. But another very important reason you need to know these attributes is because of the ambush. The things that detour you from your path now and lie in wait for you in the future are probably rooted somewhere in your earlier years. A wise man wants to know what his enemy might use against him in the battle for the grail.

Ultimately, the man God made you to be will have to wrestle the man you've become. However, the battle will not be enjoined until you begin to flesh out the differences between the two and reach the critical point at which you reject the imitation and fight for the genuine. Don't live life as a simulacrum. Reject the copy with no original and became an original with no copy.

The Chosen

Over and over in Scripture we see God choose certain men and women. The Bible uses phrases like "God chose" or "God knew" or "God's favor rested on." Nothing can compare with knowing and being known by God, and then making Him known to those we love.

But next to that, the most valuable asset you will have in this life is your hearth. In fact, the apostle Paul argued that marriage is the mystery of life most closely associated with our relationship with Christ Himself. You choose your hearth, and she responds in turn by choosing you. Something is uniquely powerful about choosing. As we discovered, choosing is inextricably linked to knowing and being known. In choosing we become known, and in knowing we choose. The problem arises when we choose before we know, which isn't fatal, but it can make things difficult. Ultimately, you will choose to protect your hearth and ensure that the flame it guards (you) does not overheat and damage the very thing that protects it (your hearth).

You also choose friends. Frankly, as we get older, we more easily choose *not* to have friends. The demands of life, our dissatisfaction with ourselves, and the difficulties we've experienced trying to find someone with whom we actually want to be friends (and who mutually wants to be friends with us) makes friendships awkward or unfulfilling. But the bottom line is this: You *must* have certain men in your life. They are indispensable to your quest. They will be the mighty men when you need allies. They will be in your corner through the tough times, helping you see the things you can't see and telling you the things you may not want to hear. And they will stand at the end of your life and tell your story. They are the witnesses to your life.

The weekend before the confirmation hearings for then Supreme Court nominee Samuel Alito, I watched a series of interviews on C-SPAN. The evening was late, and I really wanted to go to sleep, but I couldn't turn the program off as the show moved from one interview to the next. Each interview was with someone who had known the justice earlier in his life. I had recently read several news stories about him and had watched a speech several years earlier, but I didn't feel like I really knew much about the man.

When I first turned to the channel, C-SPAN was interviewing Alito's high school Latin teacher. Then they aired an interview with his high school debate team partner, followed by his classmate at Princeton, who later became Alito's roommate at Yale. None of these three were surprised one bit that Samuel Alito was a nominee for the United States Supreme Court. In fact, they seemed less surprised than Justice Alito himself. I felt as if I had learned more about the man from his friends and coworkers than I would have from a conversation with Justice Alito. Other people are much better at telling our story because they watched us discover ourselves. They helped us see the shades and hues of our life portrait that few other people would have seen.

But the way we will be known in the future is primarily through our children. They tell our story to their children, who then speak our name in the land of the living long after we are gone. The lives of our children make up the text of the greatest sermon we can ever preach. They are testaments to our character. They are our glory. Interestingly, Adam and Eve did not have children until after they sinned and were subject to death. They were no longer physically immortal. A time would come when they would leave the land of the living, so perhaps they sensed a need to project themselves into the future somehow.

Understanding Life

As I've said before, once you know about every man's quest to know and be known, things will just make more sense. You will understand more of the *why* behind the *how* people do things and say things.

You will see the desire to be known reflected in the lives of your children, your wife, and even the person bagging the groceries at the supermarket. Although they could not put a name to it, it is the thing that drives their day and many of the exchanges they have with you and with others.

For instance, if you manage people, you will discover that employees aren't as concerned with whether you implement their idea as they are that you, their supervisor, know who they are and what they said. Dismissing their ideas or suggestions without acknowledging that you are clear on what they said—or worse, not listening clearly and misunderstanding the idea—makes them feel rejected. They weren't known. The conversation didn't start out as personal, but it became personal.

Likewise, people who feel their boss has mischaracterized them feel a dissonance between who they are and who they are known to be. This is an attack on their vocation—the *thing* God intended them to do. Recognizing peoples' need to be known enables you to better understand them.

The month before our seventeenth wedding anniversary, my wife and I were able to go on a second honeymoon of sorts. Because of the thoughtfulness and generosity of a friend of my wife, we were able to go to the Dominican Republic for a week. It was a fantastic experience, and we had a great time. But we had one little complication—we don't speak Spanish.

For the most part we got by okay, but one morning as we walked out the door of our bungalow, one of the maids stopped me and, with a frustrated look on her face, pointed at a storage closet near our room. Then she started talking—in *Spanish*.

I had no idea what she was saying, so I smiled politely and then, with a concerned look, asked what I could do—in *English*. She pointed at the closet but made no move toward it. Then she spoke again—in *Spanish*.

Sensing this was somehow associated with the closet, I walked toward the door, pointed at it, and asked if she needed something from it—in *English*. But I talked *very* slowly, for some reason thinking that might help. She put her hands on her hips and started nodding her head up and down as if I was doing what she wanted, all the while talking in a *very* agitated tone—in *Spanish*.

I tried to open the door, but it was locked. I looked back at her, and she just stared at me. She paused for a minute and then made a brief comment, which went completely over my head because…it was in *Spanish*. I wiggled the door handle again and then turned back to face her, trying to use body language to say, "I have no idea what you want from me."

About that time one of her coworkers appeared, and thankfully, he spoke English. I told him the maid was trying to ask me something, and that I thought there was some sort of problem in the closet.

He talked with the maid for a moment, and then he turned back to me and said, "She just wanted to know if you have seen the key for the closet. She left it in the door a few minutes ago, and now it's gone."

I later thought back to the incident. Here were two adult human beings going about their lives right next to each other, yet when an occasion arose that required them to understand what was going on in each other's lives they had only a cryptic idea of what the other person was saying. It wasn't a big issue, just a misplaced key. But after just a few minutes of trying to engage each other I was about to walk away while mumbling to myself, *What was that all about?*

In a way, that happens to us every day—not so much because of a language problem, but because so often our language *masks* the problem. The words we say are not conveying what we really want, often because we really don't know *what* we are really trying to say. But in time you will—if you know the code. It will just take a little practice.

Engaging my quest to be known helps me understand life each and every day and in ways I would never have imagined. Admittedly, I still struggle with this journey, but it is becoming more natural all the time. Recognizing that

I am a grail helps me put my life and the things I pursue into perspective. I know my priorities. My quest flows from knowing God and being known by Him, to my hearth, to my story, to my *thing*, and to my friends. It is pretty simple. Not easy, just simple.

My quest is for the *holy* grail. At the end of the day, I want to face God and say, "I finished the course; I fought the good fight. I have been set apart as a vessel of honor for Your use." I am committed to this journey, and I am confident of the outcome. Why? Because I have a grail keeper.

I embrace the words of the apostle Paul who, near the end of his life and after years and years of hardship, said, "I *know* whom I have believed, and I am convinced that He is able to guard [keep]…what has been entrusted to me." He is my grail keeper.

Life from the Dark Places

The very first phrase in the Bible is "In the beginning." In the beginning God created the heavens and the earth, and then while darkness covered the face of the earth, God spoke into the darkness and brought order. The seeds of life that God placed in the earth were released, and the earth brought forth vegetation and all kinds of wonderful things.

But this wasn't God's beginning. It wasn't "in the beginning of God." It was *in the beginning* of the story of mankind and God's involvement with him. God existed forever *before* the universe began, and He will exist forever after the universe as we know it is no more. Instead, the beginning of this story of mankind set the broad stage of creation, and then it concentrates on what happens here—on earth. For a time the earth was in darkness, in chaos. But then God brought life to the creation He had already set in place.

Several years ago I watched a show on the Discovery Channel about geologists who study the earth by drilling deep into its surface and pulling up core samples. These extremely long, narrow poles filled with what at first looks like muck contain a cross section of the earth's surface. The rock, sand, ice, and mud are in some sort of chronological order. The idea is that the soil and material of ages past are stacked age upon age, which means the story of the earth's surface is written within it.

By studying a core sample pulled from several thousand feet under ground, scientists were able to plot the earth's temperature and weather over a considerable period of time. According to their findings, the earth experienced wild fluctuations in its weather over a period of tens of thousands of years, with periods of very high temperatures followed by periods of very low temperatures, each occurring with regularity. The graph detailed wild swings in reasonably short periods of time. The surface of the earth was, in a word, in chaos.

But according to these geologists, the temperature inexplicably stabilized, which allowed life to flourish on earth. Did the earth exist before this? Yes, but life couldn't thrive until the chaos was removed.

This is the beginning of your story. You may have been a Christian your entire life, or your faith may be a recent thing. But until you determined to engage your quest to be known, the deepest parts of your life and your soul struggled for significance. You were restless. Darkness, or sullenness, brooded over the deep, unexplored areas of God's creation—your life. But that is about to change.

Knighted

The Book of Common Prayer contains a blessing pronounced over a person as part of his baptism. As you enter what I believe will be a time of profound change for you and those around you, I would like to say a prayer for you and pronounce this blessing over you:

> Father God, as this man fully engages the life You placed in him, and in doing so begins his journey home to You, and toward the man You made him to be, I pray that You will fill him with the knowledge of Your will in all spiritual wisdom and understanding. I pray this so that he may live a life that pleases You, bear fruit in all his work, and come to know You in a profound and personal way. Strengthen him with Your own power so that he might always have the supernatural endurance, patience, and joy he needs to complete his journey.
>
> Seal this man with Your Spirit, *in token that hereafter he shall not be ashamed to confess the faith of Christ crucified, and manfully to fight under His banner...and to continue as Christ's faithful soldier and servant unto his life's end.*

Jesus said the kingdom of God is forcefully advancing, and He went on to say that the valiant man presses into it, just as an army lays siege to a city. If you are to engage this quest, you need to lean into it—to press into it.

Remember this Scripture: "Creation waits with eager longing for the revealing of the sons of God." This is not a quest you dream up; it is a quest you accept. And though, as with most quests, the journey seems uncertain and the path unclear, as you step into the gait of *know and be known*—that certain way of walking and of seeing—the quest will unfold before you. Don't just hope this is true. Expect it to be so, and you will be amazed at the ways in which you will become the man God made you to be.

Selah.

To contact Marcus Ryan about speaking at your church,
men's group, or event, visit his website at
www.marcusryan.com.

OTHER GREAT HARVEST HOUSE READING FOR MEN

10 Things I Want My Son to Know
Steve Chapman

Steve shares humorous insights, personal experience, and God-given wisdom to help fathers help their sons become men of God and men of honor. Topics include discipline's role and building skills for a successful marriage.

A Hunter Sets His Sights
Steve Chapman

From matching wits with a wily old gobbler to a heart-stopping encounter with a bull elk, Steve delivers insights and truths to help readers experience the joy of the outdoors while drawing closer to God.

A Look at Life from a Deer Stand
Steve Chapman

Taking readers on his successful and not-so-successful hunts, Chapman shares the skills for successful hunting—and living. With excitement and humor, he shares the parallels between hunting and walking with God.

God's Man of Influence
Jim George

How can a man have a life of lasting impact? Here are the secrets to having a positive and meaningful influence in the lives of everyone a man meets, including his own wife and children.

A Man After God's Own Heart
Jim George

Many Christian men want to be men after God's own heart...but how do they do this? George shows that a heartfelt desire to grow spiritually is all that's needed. God's grace does the rest.

A Husband After God's Own Heart
Jim George

Husbands will find their marriages growing richer and deeper as they pursue God and discover 12 areas in which they can make a real difference in their relationship with their wife.